Donut Mastery:

100 Saccharine Homemade Doughnut Recipes

Marissa Marie

Contents

Introduction 1
    Know Your Measurements 2
    Know Your Ingredients 4
    Know you Equipment 7
    Basics of Making Donuts 9
    Tips and Tricks 12

Basic Donut Recipes 14
    Choco-Cake Donuts 14
    Crispy Cream Donuts 16
    French Crullers 18
    Fundamental Yeast-Raised Donuts 19
    Mashed Potato Donuts 21
    Sour Cream Donuts 23
    Traditional Buttermilk Donuts 24
    Yeast-Raised Choco Donuts 26

Basic Toppings, Glazes, and Frostings 28
    Glaze Recipe 1: Crunchy Sugar Glaze 28
    Glaze Recipe 2: Soft and Sheer Sugar Glaze 29
    Glaze Recipe 3: Citrus Glaze 29
    Glaze Recipe 4: Spiced Orange Glaze 30
    Glaze Recipe 5: Cocoa Glaze 31

- Glaze Recipe 6: Dark Chocolate Glaze ... 31
- Glaze Recipe 7: Dark Chocolate Ganache Glaze ... 32
- Glaze Recipe 8: Peanut Butter Glaze ... 33
- Topping: Cinnamon-Sugar ... 34
- Frosting: Cream Cheese ... 34
- Filling: Pastry Cream ... 35

Advanced Donut Recipes ... 36
- Appamon Donuts ... 36
- Appy Donuts ... 38
- Appy Fritters ... 39
- Banana Overload Donuts ... 41
- Beignets ... 43
- Blueberry Creamy Fritters ... 45
- Brown Bonanza Donuts ... 46
- Caracanbon Donuts ... 51
- Carrot Cake Donuts ... 52
- Cheesecake Loaded Donuts ... 54
- Choco Blast Donuts ... 55
- Choco-Coated Strawberry Donuts ... 56
- Choco-Frosted Donuts ... 58
- Choco-Glazed Donut ... 59
- Chocolate Mousse Donuts ... 60

Chocomel Donuts 62

Choco-Peanut Butter Donuts 63

Choco-Sour Cream Donuts 64

Choco-Spice Donuts 66

Choco-Toffee Donuts 66

Churros Choco-dip 67

Cider-Buttermilk Donuts 69

Classical Donuts 71

Coconut Overload Donuts 72

Coffee Blast Donuts 74

Coffee Coat Donuts 77

Colourful Donuts 79

Creamy Donuts 79

Doughnut Shop Glazed Donuts 81

Espresso Overload Donuts 81

French Crullers with Grand Marnier Glaze 82

German Choco-Cake Donuts 82

Gingerbread Donuts with Lemon Glaze 83

Grape Overload Donuts 85

Honey Milk Donuts 86

Jammed Donuts 89

Jamy Donuts 90

Kid's Party Donuts	92
Lemon Blast Donuts	93
Lemon Overload Donuts	96
Macon Donuts	97
Macon Donuts	98
Maple Donuts	99
Marshnut Donuts	100
Nuteja Donuts	102
Oreo Cream Donuts	104
Peachcan Fritters	105
Peanut Jelly Donuts	106
Peppermint Mocha Donuts	109
PumpSpice Donuts	110
Radiant Vanilla Donuts	112
Raspberry-Fraîche Donuts	113
Red Velvet Donuts	115
Rich Crème Brûlée Donuts	118
Rosy French Crullers	121
S'mores Donuts	121
Saccharine Cream Donuts	123
Sizzling Cocoa Donuts	125
Smooth Chocolate Donuts	126

Snowy Choco-Truffle Donuts 128

Sugar Cinnamon Donuts 129

Sweet and Sour Donuts... 130

Sweet Potato Donuts 131

Sweet Pumpkin Donuts 133

Toasty Almond Donuts 134

Traditional Lard Donuts 136

Traditional Powdered Donuts 138

Traditional Sour Cream Cake Donuts 139

Ultra-Choco-Ganache Donuts 141

Ultra-Sweet Fritters 141

Vanilla Blast Donuts 143

Vegan Gluten-Free Baked Donuts 144

Vibrant Donuts 145

Walnaple Donuts 147

Endnote 150

Introduction

The king of comfort foods, donuts are one of the most popular snacks out there today. The pleasure of enjoying a fresh and delicious donut with a cup of coffee of tee is unrivalled. Everyone has their own favourite beverage to go with donuts though. While I personally prefer coffee, my husband likes it with tea, and my kids like to enjoy donuts with hot chocolate or milk. You're just going to have to play around with beverages too learn what beverage you like best with your donuts.

Donuts are usually rich in carbohydrates and are hence most commonly enjoyed during breakfast, to give you that much needed energy to power through the early hours of your day. I, however, like to eat these whenever I'm craving for a delicious snack.

If you're a fan of the donuts you find in the market, wait till you have mastered the art of making your own. Once you get a taste of fresh homemade donuts, those market donuts will be ruined for you forever. Homemade donuts are fresh, and you have full control over the sweetness and ingredients. You can make donuts tailored exactly to your taste, and no market donut can do that for you.

Wondering if making your own donuts is hard? I'll answer that question for you right now. Making donuts is easier than you think. If you've got an oven in your kitchen, you're good to go. Your first batch of donuts might not turn out to be the prettiest thing you've ever seen in your life, but keep at it, and with practice you will eventually make the donut of your dreams!

With the help of this book, I hope to help you make your own homemade donuts from scratch. With step-by-step instructions and helpful tips, I hope you are able to make your own donuts just like any professional baker.

Know Your Measurements

American cooks use standard containers, the 8-ounce cup and a tablespoon that takes exactly 16 level fillings to fill that cup level. Measuring by cup makes it very difficult to give weight equivalents, as the density plays an important role when it comes to weight. The easiest way therefore to deal with cup measurements in recipes is to take the amount by volume rather than by weight. Thus, the equation reads:

1 cup = 240ml = 8 fluid Ounces

½ cup = 120ml = 4 fluid ounces

It is possible to buy a set of American cup measures in major stores around the world.

In the States, butter is sometimes measured in sticks. One stick is the equivalent of 8 tablespoons. One tablespoon of butter is therefore the equivalent to ½ ounce/15 grams.

Liquid Measures

1 Teaspoon= 5 Millilitres

1 Tablespoon = 14 millilitres

2 Tablespoons= 1 Fluid Ounce

Solid Measures

1 Ounce= 28 Grams

16 Ounces= 1 Pound

For dry ingredients, high-quality stainless-steel cups and spoons that are sturdy enough not to dent (dents make for inaccurate measurements), such as those made by Cuisipro work great. The dip and sweep method works great for measuring sugar and flour. Whisk the flour first to aerate it, then dip and sweep the top even with the back of a knife.

For liquid measurements, the standard Pyrex measuring cups available at most supermarkets and kitchenware stores work fine. Always try to use a cup similar to the amount you are measuring. For example, never use a 4-cup measuring cup to measure out ½ cup of liquid.

Know Your Ingredients

Ingredients are the most important part of a recipe. Better, fresher ingredients result in a better tasting recipe.

BUTTER: Use fresh unsalted butter.

SUGAR: When a recipe has just sugar listed as an ingredient, it means regular granulated sugar.

Light and dark brown sugar: These must be tightly packed into precise measuring cups.

Confectioners' sugar: Also known as powdered sugar, this should be sifted before measurement.

Colored sugars, sprinkles/jimmies, and sugar decorations: These come in multiple shapes and sizes, and can be easily sourced from cake-decorating supply stores.

EGGS: Use eggs graded "large."

FLOUR: Multiple types of flours are listed as ingredients in multiple recipes. King Arthur Unbleached All-Purpose Flour is a great all-purpose flour. Softasilk is a good choice for a cake flour.

Baking soda and baking powder: It is better to use fresh baking soda and baking powder. Doubleacting baking powder works great in every recipe in this book.

Yeast: Make sure the yeast is not expired. Fresher yeast is always better. I don't like to use instant yeast in my recipes as it can reduce raising times to almost half. Red Star active dry yeast works great. Try it out!

Salt: All recipes in this book call for regular table salt. If you're using a different kind of salt, you will need to slightly adjust the measurement.

Milk, Cream Cheese, Sour Cream: Full-Fat versions are best for making doughnuts.

Heavy Cream: Cream labelled as "heavy" works much better than cream labelled as "whipping" for making donuts.

Extracts: Natural is always better. Use pure vanilla and almond extracts, instead of those containing artificial flavours.

Citrus Zests: Always use just the colored part of the zest and never the bitter white pith that lies beneath. Use a Microplane zester for best results.

Bittersweet and semisweet chocolate: If you're just starting out making donuts, I'll advise you to use the type of chocolate I've listed. Once you get the hang of making donuts, feel free to swap the types of chocolates around to your heart's content. As for the brands of these chocolates you can buy from the market, Ghirardelli and Callebaut work great. For specialty chocolates, Valrhona and Scharffen Berger are great options.

Milk chocolate: I like Callebaut, Scharffen Berger, Ghirardelli, and Valrhona.

White chocolate: White chocolates that list cocoa butter in the ingredients instead of palm or other oils taste best when used in donuts. Brands to buy are- Callebaut and Valrhona.

Unsweetened Cocoa Powder: There are multiple kinds of these available in the market today. The recipes in this book call for both- Dutch-processed cocoa powder and natural cocoa powder. Check the label and make sure you use the right one.

Nuts: It is vitally important to use fresh nuts in donuts. Keep your nuts fresh by placing them in air-tight containers and storing them in a freezer or refrigerator.

Coconut: Some of the recipes in this book list 100 percent unsweetened coconut milk as an ingredient. This can be found in the Asian section of most large supermarkets or in Asian food stores. Other recipes list sweetened long-shred coconut as an ingredient, which can be found in any supermarket baking aisle.

Spices: Never use stale spices. It usually takes about 6 months on the shelf for spices to get stale, so keep that in mind. All recipes use ground spices, unless otherwise specified.

Oil And Frying Fats: Fried donuts make up a large share of the donut recipes in this book. What you choose to fry your donuts in can make a huge difference. It is important for the frying fat to be deep enough to thoroughly deep-fry the donuts. Personally, I like to use canola oil, but feel free to use an oil of your preference that can get the job done. It is important for the oil to be clean, and discard the oil after frying two or three batches of donuts. Usually, it is time to change the oil when it contains too many particles of the past batches, or it smells off.

Know you Equipment

There are tools for every trade. Sure, you could find ways to complete the task without dedicated tools, but if you're in this for the long haul, it is best to invest in tools that will make your life much easier.

Pastry Bag, Coupler, and Tips: Quite a few of the recipes in this book will require the use of pastry bags and decorating tips. Some of the tips require a coupler to attach to the pastry bag, while others can be directly inserted into a pastry bag. For example, Ateco #847 can be directly inserted into the pastry bag. (search amazon.com for "Ateco #847" to find and buy it if you can't in a nearby store). For filling doughnuts with jelly, jam, or custard, Ateco #230 Bismarck tip does a great job. This tip has a sharp, slanted opening, perfect for inserting into doughnuts and creating a channel for your filling. (search amazon.com for "Ateco #230" to find and buy it if you can't in a nearby store)

Deep-Fat Fryer: Although not necessary, a dedicated electric deep-fryer can make your life much easier. Check out the 1800 watt "Waring Pro deep-fat fryer" on amazon. It is perfect for making donuts and even French fried!

Heavy, Deep Pot: If you're on a budget, and don't wish to invest in an electrical deep fryer, all you really need is a heavy pot deep enough to hold at least 3 inches of oil/fat, and should be wide enough to hold plenty of donuts simultaneously. Most kitchens have such a vessel available, but if yours doesn't, consider investing in a triple-ply stainless-steel or an anodized aluminum pot.

Thermometer: An accurate thermometer can make your life much easier. From oil temperature to water temperature for proofing yeast, a thermometer will do it all. The "Maverick CT-

03 digital oil and candy thermometer" does the job quite well. Check it out on amazon.

Electric Mixer: An electric mixer makes the job easier and faster. If you have the time and patience, a hand mixer will do the job too.

Food Processor: Any decent food processor will do. Go to amazon.com and get one that had good review, and is in your budget.

Microwave Oven: Microwaves are best for melting dark chocolate and butter. The time it will take for your microwave to get the job done will depend on its wattage. You might want to play around and experiment a little to learn how long your microwave takes to to a particular job.

Jellyroll Pans/Rimmed Baking Sheet Pans: Heavyweight aluminium or stainless-steel rimmed sheet pans, also called rimmed baking sheet pans, will do the job.

Doughnut Cutters: If you're serious about making donuts, you will need to invest in a specialized donut cutter, which will help you make the classic ring-shaped donuts. There are plenty of these available on amazon and in local stores. If you want to make donuts of shapes other than the ring, you have plenty of options available for that too.

Doughnut Pans: These are used in quite a few of the recipes in this book. These are used to hold softer dough which cannot be shaped using a cutter. There are plenty of these available on amazon, and in local markets.

Basics of Making Donuts

If you've never made a donut in your life, this section is vital for you. If you have made donuts in the past, read this section anyway, and maybe you will learn something new.

Forming Donuts

By default, I like to roll the dough to a ½-inch thickness. If not specified in a recipe, you can never go wrong with the ½ inch-thickness roll. If you have never rolled dough before, learn to do it. You will require a slightly floured work surface, unless otherwise specified in the recipe. Handle the dough carefully and gently, making sure the texture remains intact. A ruler can be very useful to measure the thickness of the dough. In time, you will learn to estimate the thickness with reasonable accuracy, but until then, use a ruler. Once you're done with the initial cuts using a floured cutter, carefully gather the dough, reroll, and cut again. Rolling the dough for a third time can make the dough a little stiff, so do it only if you absolutely have to.

Filling Donuts Before Frying

Filling the doughnuts before frying can come in handy for quite a few of the recipes. The filling is usually sticky before frying, which makes it the ideal time to pipe. Filling donuts before frying can also come in handy when there are multiple fillings, and when the filling is too chunky to flow through a pastry tip. Roll the risen yeast dough out to a ¼-inch thickness and divide into an even number of 2½-inch rounds. Dollop the filling into the centers of half of the rounds. Brush the edges of the filled rounds using water. Top with the other rounds and seal the edges tightly by strongly applying pressure to every part of the edge using your fingers. Allow to rise a second time. Once risen, the seam will be invisible!

Choosing Your Frying Fat

You need an oil that has a high smoking point. In other words, you need an oil that stays stable at high temperatures during deep frying. Canola oil, safflower oil, sunflower oil, and grape-seed oil work great. Corn oil and peanut oil are also good for frying but have strong flavour and can add it to the donut recipe. If however, you're making donuts with these flavours, feel free to add them. Oil can last to make to about 3 batches of one recipe. Never use oil used for one recipe for making another recipe.

Frying Donuts

As mentioned before, an electric fryer makes things easier, but you can also fry your donuts in a traditional way. The oil in the fryer should be at least 3 inches deep, and there should be a couple of inches of headspace too. The container should be wide enough to hold at least 3 doughnuts simultaneously.

Once your frying equipment is good and ready, it is time to ready your work area. You will need two rimmed baking sheet pans lined with three coverings of paper towels. Paper towels go even better over racks, as the surplus oil can drip down.

Make sure that all of your doughnuts are free of excess flour before frying. If there is excess flour, use a soft, dry pastry brush to brush it off.

Once the donut is ready to throw into the fryer, you have a few options. If the donut is firm enough, you can just throw them into the fryer using your fingers. If the donut starts to break as you pick it up, this is not the best technique. If your fingers don't work, you will need to use a spatula. Coat a spatula big enough to hold a donut with oil, slip it under the donut, pick it up, and then lower it into the fryer.

In each recipe, I mention the frying time and frying temperature, but these will vary with the size of the donut and other factors like room temperature, and the temperature of the ingredients. You will need to make a few matches to get a hang of the time and temperature. Temperature is easy to maintain if you're using an electric fryer. You will need to constantly check the temperature and make adjustments accordingly if you're using a stovetop fryer.

The time you fry the donut is of vital importance. Fry it for too long, and you get a dry donut. Fry it for less than ideal time and you get an undercooked donut. Visual cues are important to tell when a donut is done. Learn these as even a few seconds could be the difference between a dry, undercooked, and perfect donut. A few of the donuts are dark by default and don't exhibit much change upon frying. In case of these donuts, you will just need to rely on estimation. Whenever in doubt, make a test batch before you go all in.

Once your donuts are fried, take them out of the fryer and place them over paper towels to drain. Wait ten seconds, then flip them over onto a dry portion of the paper to drain for another ten seconds. Some of the ingredients like powdered sugars are best added to the donut in this phase, so make sure you have them ready. Glazes can be applied to the donut when it has cooled considerably, but still a little warm. Allow your donuts to cool completely before filling them with dairy bases fillings.

Baking Donuts

If you want your donuts to really look perfect, it is best to use doughnut pans. These are available in both standard and small size. The standard size pan has been used in the recipes in this book.

Filling Donuts After Frying

A long, narrow pastry tip, called a Bismarck tip is ideal for injecting the filling into the donut. All you need to do is fill a pastry bag, fit a Bismarck tip to it, inject the tip halfway into the donut, and then squeeze. The contents of the pastry bag will flow into the donut. Keep squeezing as you withdraw the tip. If you want a donut with high density filling, insert the tip, wiggle it around in a circular motion to make an air pocket, then squeeze the bag to insert the filling.

Glazing and Frosting Donuts

There are multiple kinds of glazes available out there , and quite a few of these have been used in this book. It is best to prepare the glaze immediately before using it, and placing it in a container big enough to incorporate a whole doughnut with your fingers around it. Take one slightly warm doughnut at a time, hold it by its sides, and immerse a broad side of it into the glaze. Press it lightly into the glaze so that it comes at least halfway up the sides of the doughnut. Gently rotate the doughnut as you remove it from the glaze, turning it upright and placing it on a rack or baking sheet to dry. Both firm and soft glazes will improve from a short rest. They will lose a bit of their stickiness, making them easier to handle and eat. If the glaze starts to harden in the bowl while you are still working with it, just whisk it until smooth or reheat it. This is not the only way to apply the glaze. You can also pour it over a donut using a ladle or spoon.

Applying Dry Coatings

Powders like Cinnamon sugar and confectioners' sugar are needed to be applied to the donuts for quite a few recipes in this book. These are best applied when the donut is still warm, but not too hot or cold. Feel free to apply multiple coatings until your desired amount has been applied.

Tips and Tricks

Before we get into the recipes, let us take a final look at some tips and tricks.

- Oil temperature is important. An electrical fryer regulates the temperature for you, but if you don't have one, you will have to do it manually.
- Baking times will vary with the thickness and size you cut your donuts. If you cut your donuts to exactly the sizes mentioned in the recipes, the cooking times should be exactly the same, assuming other factors are reasonably same. If your donut is undercooked or overcooked, tweak the timing in the next batch.
- If you're trying a new recipe, make a test batch before going all in with multiple doughnuts. One ruined donut is better than three.
- Paper towels are awesome. Make sure you have plenty of them before making a batch of donuts. Use these to remove as much oil from the donuts as you can before serving.

- Donuts are best enjoyed fresh! Saving donuts for later can take away most of their initial juiciness and flavour. Make only as much as you can eat!

Basic Donut Recipes

There are a few base donuts that are used in multiple recipes that follow. You would do well to master these recipes, and know where they are when a recipe later in the book calls for them.

Choco-Cake Donuts

Another donut for chocolate lovers!
Yield: about fourteen 3-inch doughnuts
Ingredients:
- ¼ cup flavorless vegetable oil, such as canola
- ½ cup sifted Dutch-processed cocoa powder
- ½ teaspoon baking soda
- 1 cup buttermilk, at room temperature
- 1 cup plus 2 tablespoons sifted cake flour
- 1 cup sugar
- 1 tablespoon baking powder
- 1 tablespoon pure vanilla extract
- 1 teaspoon salt
- 2 ounces semisweet chocolate (not more than 55% cacao), such as Callebaut or Ghirardelli
- 2½ cups all-purpose flour
- 3 large eggs, at room temperature
- Flavorless vegetable oil for deep-frying, such as canola

Directions:
1. Mix together both flours, the cocoa, baking powder, salt, and baking soda in a big container.
2. Heat the oil and chocolate together in a microwave or the top of a double boiler until the chocolate melts. Whisk until smooth; turn off the heat and cool slightly.

3. Using a separate big container, blend the sugar and eggs using an electric mixer until pale and creamy, or mix thoroughly using your hands. Put in and mix in the vanilla along with the melted chocolate mixture, then put in the buttermilk and beat until well blended. Put in the dry mixture in two batches and mix using a wooden spoon only until the dough comes together. The dough will be fairly soft. Cover and place in the fridge for minimum 2 hours or up to overnight.
4. Cover a rimmed baking sheet pan with a layer of three paper towels. Heat up 3 inches of oil using a deep pot or deep-fat fryer to 350° to 355°F.
5. As the oil heats, dust the work surface generously with flour. Scrape half of the dough onto the surface, coat the top of the dough slightly with flour, and roll the dough until it is ½ inch thick. Cut out donuts using a slightly floured 3-inch round cutter. Slowly gather all the left-over dough, press it together, roll the dough again to the same thickness, and cut out as many additional donuts as you possibly can. Repeat the process with the rest of the dough.
6. Fry multiple donuts simultaneously, without crowding. Fry for approximately 1 minute and 40 seconds, turn the donuts over, and fry for approximately 1 minute and 40 seconds more on the other side, until just cooked through. (See Doughnut Tip.) With the help of a slotted spoon, take each donut out of the fryer and drain well using paper towels. Repeat the process for the rest of the donuts.
7. Top with dry toppings and glaze to taste.

Crispy Cream Donuts

A light, spongy, sweet, sticky, and insanely delicious donut!
Yield: about twenty-six 2½-inch round doughnuts or about twenty-two 3-inch ring-shaped doughnuts

Ingredients:
- ¼ cup warm water (110° to 115°F)
- 6 tablespoons vegetable shortening, such as Crisco
- 1½ cups whole milk
- ½ cup sugar
- 2 large eggs, at room temperature, beaten
- 1 teaspoon salt
- 1 teaspoon freshly grated nutmeg
- 1 teaspoon pure vanilla extract
- 5 to 5½ cups all-purpose flour
- Flavorless vegetable oil for deep-frying, such as canola
- 2 0.25-ounce packages active dry yeast

Directions:
1. Place the warm water in a big container and sprinkle the yeast over it. Stir to combine and allow to sit for 5 minutes.
2. In the meantime, melt the shortening with the milk in a microwave or in a saucepan on the stovetop, then cool to lukewarm (110° to 115°F). Put in the milk mixture, sugar, eggs, salt, nutmeg, vanilla, and 2½ cups of the flour to the yeast and mix using a wooden spoon or silicone spatula until well blended and smooth. The mixture will have some body but will still be very wet and loose. Add mix in another 2½ cups of the flour until the mixture becomes a very slightly sticky, elastic dough, adding more of the remaining ½ cup flour only if needed. Knead thoroughly by beating rapidly using a the spoon or spatula, or use a stand mixer with the flat paddle or dough hook attachment.

3. Put the dough in a buttered container, leaving plenty of headroom. Cover the container using plastic wrap and place in a warm, draft-free location to rise until twice its initial size, approximately 1 hour.
4. Thoroughly flour two rimmed baking sheet pans. Softly punch down the dough and split it in half. Roll one piece of dough on a slightly floured work surface to ½-inch thickness. Cut out doughnuts with a slightly floured cutter. Use a 2½-inch round cutter for filled doughnuts or a 3-inch ring-shaped doughnut cutter for a classic doughnut shape. Repeat the process with the rest of the dough. Slowly gather all the left-over dough, press it together, roll the dough again to the same thickness, and cut out as many additional donuts as you possibly can. Place the doughnuts, well spaced, on the prepared pans. Allow to rise in a warm, draft-free location until twice its initial size, approximately half an hour.
5. Coat two rimmed baking sheet pans with a layer of three paper towels. Heat up 3 inches of oil using a deep pot or deep-fat fryer to 350° to 355°F. Once the oil has reached the desired temperature, fry a few doughnuts at a time; do not crowd. Fry until your donuts become slightly golden brown, approximately 1½ minutes, turn the donuts over, and fry for approximately 1½ minutes more, until the other side looks slightly golden-brown too. With the help of a slotted spoon, take each donut out of the fryer and drain well using paper towels. Repeat the process for the rest of the donuts.
6. Apply dry toppings or glaze, or fill as you wish.

French Crullers

A donut with the goodness of the classis French choux paste!
Yield: about nine 3-inch crullers
Ingredients:
- ½ cup (1 stick) unsalted butter, at room temperature, cut into pieces
- ½ cup plus 2 tablespoons water
- ½ cup plus 2 tablespoons whole milk
- 1 cup all-purpose flour
- 1 teaspoon salt
- 1 teaspoon sugar
- 3 large eggs, at room temperature
- Flavorless vegetable oil for deep-frying, such as canola
- Pastry bag fitted with a large star decorating tip (such as Ateco #847)

Directions:
1. Cut nine 5-inch squares of parchment paper, lay them on 2 rimmed baking sheet pans, and grease them liberally using non-stick cooking spray. Cover a separate rimmed baking sheet pan with a layer of three paper towels.
2. Mix the water, milk, butter, salt, and sugar in a moderate sized saucepan on moderate-high heat. Bring to a rolling boil; turn off the heat.
3. Rapidly mix in the flour all at once until the batter comes together. Place over very low heat and mix until the dough becomes dry, 1 minute or less. The mixture should come away cleanly from the sides of the saucepan. Place the dough in the container of a stand mixer with the paddle attachment.
4. Switch the mixture on to moderate speed and put in the eggs one at a time, making sure one is completely

blended before you put in another. The batter should be smooth and stiff enough to retain a shape when mounded with a spoon.

5. Put the dough into the pastry bag. Pipe a 3-inch ring over each parchment square. It is ok if the ends of the ring overlap a little. If the end sticks to the pastry tip, use kitchen scissors to cut it free.
6. Heat up 3 inches of oil using a deep pot or deep-fat fryer to 350° to 355°F. Once the oil has reached the desired temperature, pick up one parchment square at a time and cautiously but quickly invert it so that the cruller slides into the oil (take care not to allow your fingers to touch the hot oil). Fry multiple donuts simultaneously, without crowding. Fry until you see the donuts get a golden-brown colour, approximately 2 minutes , turn the donuts over, and fry for approximately 2 minutes more, until you see the donuts get the golden-brown colour on the other side too. With the help of a slotted spoon, Take each donut out of the oil and drain well using paper towels. Repeat the process for the rest of the donuts.
7. Top with dry toppings and glaze to taste.

Fundamental Yeast-Raised Donuts

These donuts are raised using yeast, and are form a spongy and light base for your favourite topping!
Yield: about twenty-eight 2½-inch round doughnuts or about twenty-four 3-inch ring-shaped doughnuts
Ingredients:

- ⅔ cup warm water (110° to 115°F)
- ¼ cup (½ stick) unsalted butter, at room temperature, cut into pieces

- ⅔ cup whole milk
- ⅔ cup sugar
- 2 large eggs, at room temperature, beaten
- 1½ teaspoons salt
- 1 teaspoon freshly grated nutmeg
- 1 teaspoon pure vanilla extract
- 5 to 5¼ cups all-purpose flour
- Flavorless vegetable oil for deep-frying, such as canola
- 2 0.25-ounce packages active dry yeast

Directions:

1. Place the warm water in a big container and sprinkle the yeast over it. Stir to combine and allow to sit for 5 minutes.
2. In the meantime, melt the butter with the milk in a microwave or in a saucepan on the stovetop, then cool to lukewarm (110° to 115°F). Put in the milk mixture, sugar, eggs, salt, nutmeg, vanilla, and 2½ cups of the flour to the yeast and mix using a wooden spoon or silicone spatula until well blended and smooth. The mixture will have some body but will still be very wet and loose. Put in another 2½ cups of the flour and mix until the mixture becomes a very slightly sticky, elastic dough, adding more of the remaining ¼ cup flour only if needed. Knead thoroughly by beating rapidly using a the spoon or spatula, or use a stand mixer with the flat paddle or dough hook attachment. The mixture should be elastic, yet somewhat sticky and not dry.
3. Put the dough in a buttered container, leaving plenty of headroom. Cover the container using plastic wrap and place in a warm, draft-free location to rise until twice its initial size, approximately 1 hour.
4. Thoroughly flour two rimmed baking sheet pans. Softly punch down the dough and split it in half. Roll one piece

of dough on a slightly floured work surface to ½-inch thickness. Cut out doughnuts with a slightly floured cutter. Use a 2½-inch round cutter for filled doughnuts or a 3-inch ring-shaped doughnut cutter for a classic doughnut shape. Repeat the process with the rest of the dough. Slowly gather all the left-over dough, press it together, roll the dough again to the same thickness, and cut out as many additional donuts as you possibly can. Place the doughnuts, well spaced, on the prepared pans. Allow to rise in a warm, draft-free location until twice its initial size, approximately half an hour.
5. Coat two rimmed baking sheet pans with a layer of three paper towels. Heat up 3 inches of oil using a deep pot or deep-fat fryer to 350° to 355°F. Once the oil has reached the desired temperature, fry a few doughnuts at a time; do not crowd. Fry until your donuts become slightly golden brown, approximately 1½ minutes, turn the donuts over, and fry for approximately 1½ minutes more, until the other side looks slightly golden-brown too. With the help of a slotted spoon, take each donut out of the fryer and drain well using paper towels. Repeat the process for the rest of the donuts.
6. Apply dry toppings, fill, or glaze as you wish.

Mashed Potato Donuts

A simple recipe, a plain canvas with soft and crunchy texture. Try it with your favourite glaze!

Yield: about eighteen 3-inch doughnuts

Ingredients:

- ¼ cup (½ stick) unsalted butter, melted and cooled
- ½ cup whole milk, at room temperature
- 1 ⅓ cups sugar
- 1 cup sifted cake flour

- 1 tablespoon baking powder
- 2 cups lightly packed baked starchy baking potato, cooled (take a starchy potato, like a russet, and either bake it or microwave it on the "baked potato" setting. Then use a pastry blender to mash it thoroughly)
- 2 teaspoons freshly grated nutmeg
- 2 teaspoons pure vanilla extract
- 2 teaspoons salt
- 3 cups all-purpose flour
- 4 large eggs, at room temperature
- Flavorless vegetable oil for deep-frying, such as canola

Directions:

1. Mix together both flours, the baking powder, and salt in a big container .
2. Using a separate big container, blend the sugar and eggs using an electric mixer until pale and creamy, or mix thoroughly using your hands. Put in and mix in the potatoes, butter, milk, nutmeg, and vanilla just until well blended. Put in the dry mixture in two batches and mix using a wooden spoon only until the dough comes together. Cover and place in the fridge for minimum 2 hours or up to overnight.
3. Take the dough out of the fridge. Cover a rimmed baking sheet pan with a layer of three paper towels. Heat up 3 inches of oil using a deep pot or deep-fat fryer to 350° to 355°F.
4. As the oil heats, lightly cover the work surface with flour. Place the dough on the readied surface, coat the top of the dough slightly with flour, and roll the dough until it is ½ inch thick. Cut out donuts using a slightly floured 3-inch round cutter. Slowly gather all the left-over dough, press it together, roll the dough again to the same thickness, and cut out as many additional donuts as you possibly can.

5. Fry multiple donuts simultaneously, without crowding. Fry until your donuts become slightly golden brown, should take around 75 seconds, turn the donuts over, and fry for around 75 seconds once again, until the other side looks slightly golden-brown too. With the help of a slotted spoon, take each donut out of the fryer and drain well using paper towels. Repeat the process for the rest of the donuts.
6. Top with dry toppings and glaze to taste.

Sour Cream Donuts

Sour cream gives these donuts a velvety texture. These form a great base for the topping and glaze of your choice.

Yield: about twelve 3-inch doughnuts

Ingredients:
- ½ teaspoon baking soda
- ½ teaspoon freshly grated nutmeg
- 1 cup full-fat sour cream, at room temperature
- 1 cup sifted cake flour
- 1 cup sugar
- 1 tablespoon baking powder
- 1 teaspoon salt
- 1½ teaspoons pure vanilla extract
- 2 large eggs, at room temperature
- 2½ cups all-purpose flour
- 5 tablespoons unsalted butter, melted and cooled
- Flavorless vegetable oil for deep-frying, such as canola

Directions:
1. Mix together both flours, the baking powder, baking soda, and salt in a big container .
2. Using a separate big container, blend the sugar and eggs using an electric mixer until pale and creamy, or

mix thoroughly using your hands. Put in and mix in the sour cream, butter, vanilla, and nutmeg until well blended. Put in the dry mixture in two batches and mix using a wooden spoon only until the dough comes together. Cover and place in the fridge for minimum 2 hours or up to overnight.
3. Take the dough out of the fridge. Cover a rimmed baking sheet pan with a layer of three paper towels. Heat up 3 inches of oil using a deep pot or deep-fat fryer to 350° to 355°F.
4. As the oil heats, lightly cover the work surface with flour. Place the dough on the readied surface, coat the top of the dough slightly with flour, and roll the dough until it is ½ inch thick. Cut out donuts using a slightly floured 3-inch round cutter. Slowly gather all the left-over dough, press it together, roll the dough again to the same thickness, and cut out as many additional donuts as you possibly can.
5. Fry multiple donuts simultaneously, without crowding. Fry until your donuts become slightly golden brown, should take around 75 seconds, turn the donuts over, and fry for around 75 seconds once again, until the other side looks slightly golden-brown too. With the help of a slotted spoon, take each donut out of the fryer and drain well using paper towels. Repeat the process with the rest of the dough.
6. Top with dry toppings and glaze to taste.

Traditional Buttermilk Donuts

Enjoy these vanilla flavoured donuts with soft texture instantly after preparing.
Yield: about sixteen 3-inch doughnuts
Ingredients:

1 TB lemon juice then milk

- 1 cup buttermilk, at room temperature
- 1 cup sugar
- 1 tablespoon pure vanilla extract
- 1 teaspoon baking soda
- 1 teaspoon freshly grated nutmeg
- 1½ cups sifted cake flour *— remove 3 TB flour, add 3 TB cornstarch*
- 1½ teaspoons salt
- 2 large eggs, at room temperature
- 2 teaspoons baking powder
- 3 cups all-purpose flour
- 6 tablespoons (¾ stick) unsalted butter, melted and cooled
- Flavorless vegetable oil for deep-frying, such as canola

Directions:

1. Mix together both flours, the baking powder, baking soda, and salt in a big container.
2. Using a separate big container, blend the sugar and eggs using an electric mixer until pale and creamy, or mix thoroughly using your hands. Put in and mix in the buttermilk, butter, vanilla, and nutmeg until well blended. Put in the dry mixture in two batches and mix using a wooden spoon only until the dough comes together. Cover and place in the fridge for minimum 2 hours or up to overnight.
3. Take the dough out of the fridge. Cover a rimmed baking sheet pan with a layer of three paper towels. Heat up 3 inches of oil using a deep pot or deep-fat fryer to 350° to 355°F.
4. As the oil heats, lightly cover the work surface with flour. Place the dough on the readied surface, coat the top of the dough slightly with flour, and roll the dough until it is ½ inch thick. Cut out donuts using a slightly floured 3-inch round cutter. Slowly gather all the left-over dough, press it together, roll the dough again to

the same thickness, and cut out as many additional donuts as you possibly can.
5. Fry multiple donuts simultaneously, without crowding. Fry until your donuts become slightly golden brown, should take around 75 seconds, turn the donuts over, and fry for around 75 seconds once again, until the other side looks slightly golden-brown too. With the help of a slotted spoon, take each donut out of the fryer and drain well using paper towels. Repeat the process for the rest of the donuts.
6. Top with dry toppings and glaze to taste.

Yeast-Raised Choco Donuts

Enjoy this soft and light chocolate donut instantly after preparing.
Yield: about twenty-four 2½-inch round doughnuts or about twenty-one 3-inch ring-shaped doughnuts
Ingredients:
- ¼ cup whole milk
- ½ cup sifted Dutchprocessed cocoa powder
- ½ cup warm water (110° to 115°F)
- ⅔ cup sugar
- 2 0.25-ounce packages active dry yeast
- 2 large egg yolks, at room temperature, beaten
- 2 teaspoons pure vanilla extract
- 2 teaspoons salt
- 4 large eggs, at room temperature, beaten
- 4 to 4½ cups all-purpose flour
- 6 tablespoons (¾ stick) unsalted butter, at room temperature, cut into pieces
- Flavorless vegetable oil for deep-frying, such as canola

Directions:

1. Mix together 4 cups of the flour and the cocoa in a big container . Place the warm water in another big container and sprinkle the yeast over it. Stir to combine and allow to sit for 5 minutes.
2. In the meantime, melt the butter with the milk in a microwave or in a saucepan on the stovetop, then cool to lukewarm (110° to 115°F). Put in the milk mixture, sugar, whole eggs, egg yolks, salt, vanilla, and half of the flour mixture to the yeast and mix using a wooden spoon or silicone spatula until well blended and smooth. The mixture will have some body but will still be very wet and loose. Add mix in the remaining flour mixture until the dough becomes a very slightly sticky, elastic dough, adding the remaining ½ cup flour only if needed. Knead thoroughly by beating rapidly using a the spoon or spatula, or use a stand mixer with the flat paddle or dough hook attachment. The mixture should be elastic, yet slightly sticky and not dry.
3. Put the dough in a buttered container, leaving plenty of headroom. Cover the container using plastic wrap and place in a warm, draft-free location to rise until twice its initial size, approximately 1 hour 15 minutes.
4. Thoroughly flour two rimmed baking sheet pans. Softly punch down the dough and split it in half. Roll one piece of dough on a slightly floured work surface to ½-inch thickness. Cut out doughnuts with a slightly floured cutter. Use a 2½-inch round cutter for filled doughnuts or a 3-inch ring-shaped doughnut cutter for a classic doughnut shape. Repeat the process with the rest of the dough. Slowly gather all the left-over dough, press it together, roll the dough again to the same thickness, and cut out as many additional donuts as you possibly can. Place the doughnuts, well spaced, on the prepared

pans. Allow to rise in a warm, draft-free location until twice its initial size, about 45 minutes.
5. Coat two rimmed baking sheet pans with a layer of three paper towels. Heat up 3 inches of oil using a deep pot or deep-fat fryer to 350° to 355°F. Once the oil has reached the desired temperature, fry a few doughnuts at a time; do not crowd. Fry for approximately 1½ minutes, turn the donuts over, and fry for approximately 1½ minutes more on the other side, until just cooked through. With the help of a slotted spoon, take each donut out of the fryer and drain well using paper towels. Repeat the process for the rest of the donuts.
6. Apply dry toppings or glaze, or fill as you wish.

Basic Toppings, Glazes, and Frostings

These basic toppings, Glazes, and frostings are used in multiple recipes that follow. You would do well to master these, and know where they are in this book.

Glaze Recipe 1: Crunchy Sugar Glaze

As the name suggests, this glaze hardens and results in a crunchy donut.

Yield: enough to coat the tops of about twelve 3-inch doughnuts

Ingredients:
- 2 cups sifted confectioners' sugar
- 2 tablespoons water

Directions:

1. Place the confectioners' sugar in a moderate-sized sauce-pan.
2. Mix in the water until it begins to blend; it will be thick before you heat it.
3. Cook over moderate heat, whisking frequently, until it liquefies and becomes totally smooth and very warm—but not hot—to the touch. Do not allow it to simmer. The cooking will be brief—approximately 15 seconds.
4. Turn off the heat and use instantly.

Glaze Recipe 2: Soft and Sheer Sugar Glaze

This is not a donut recipe. This is the recipe of a sweet soft sugar glaze for which goes will with any donut!

Yield: enough to coat the tops of about twelve 3-inch doughnuts

Ingredients:
- 2 cups sifted confectioners' sugar
- 3 to 4 tablespoons water

Directions:
1. Place the confectioners' sugar in a moderate-sized container.
2. Mix in the water a little bit at a time, until the desired consistency is reached. Use instantly.

Glaze Recipe 3: Citrus Glaze

This glaze is sweet and has a citrus hint to it.

Yield: enough to coat the tops of about twelve 3-inch doughnuts

Ingredients:
- 2 cups sifted confectioners' sugar

- 3 to 4 tablespoons freshly squeezed lemon juice, lime juice, or orange juice

Directions:
1. Place the confectioners' sugar in a moderate-sized container.
2. Mix in the citrus juice a little at a time until the desired consistency is achieved. Use instantly.

Glaze Recipe 4: Spiced Orange Glaze

This glaze has a strong citrus flavour and a hint of cinnamon and ginger.

Yield: enough to coat the tops of about twelve 3-inch doughnuts

Ingredients:
- ½ teaspoon ground ginger
- 1 teaspoon ground cinnamon
- 2 cups sifted confectioners' sugar
- 2 tablespoons freshly squeezed orange juice, or more as needed

Directions:
1. Place the confectioners' sugar and spices in a moderate-sized saucepan.
2. Mix in the orange juice until it begins to combine; it will be thick before you heat it. Cook over moderate heat, stirring continuously, until it liquefies and becomes totally smooth and very warm—but not hot—to the touch. Do not allow it to simmer. The cooking will be brief—approximately 15 seconds.
3. Turn off the heat and use instantly.

Glaze Recipe 5: Cocoa Glaze

Use this glaze on your donut if you're looking for a crunchy chocolaty donut!

Yield: enough to coat the tops of about fifteen 3-inch doughnuts

Ingredients:

- ½ cup sifted natural or Dutch-processed cocoa powder
- 3 cups sifted confectioners' sugar
- 6 tablespoons water, or more as needed

Directions:

1. Place the confectioners' sugar and cocoa in a moderate-sized saucepan.
2. Mix in the water until it begins to combine; it will be thick before you heat it.
3. Cook over moderate heat, whisking continuously, until it liquefies and becomes totally smooth and very warm—but not hot—to the touch. Do not allow it to simmer. The cooking will be brief—approximately 15 seconds.
4. Turn off the heat and use instantly.

Glaze Recipe 6: Dark Chocolate Glaze

Try this glaze I you're a fan of dark chocolate!

Yield: enough to coat the tops of about twelve 3-inch doughnuts

Ingredients:

- ¼ cup heavy cream
- 2 cups sifted confectioners' sugar
- 2 tablespoons water

- 3 ounces unsweetened chocolate, finely chopped

Directions:
1. Place the chocolate, cream, and water in a moderate sized saucepan and cook over low heat, stirring intermittently, until the chocolate is melted and the mixture is thick but smooth.
2. Mix in the confectioners' sugar and cook over medium-low heat, stirring continuously, until the mix-ture is totally smooth and very warm—but not hot—to the touch. Do not allow it to simmer. The cooking will be brief—30 seconds to 1 minute.
3. Turn off the heat and use instantly.

Glaze Recipe 7: Dark Chocolate Ganache Glaze

This chocolate glaze has a rich taste and shiny texture due to the added butter.

Yield: enough to coat the tops of about twenty 3-inch doughnuts

Ingredients:
- 1 cup heavy cream
- 1 tablespoon unsalted butter
- 10 ounces semisweet or bittersweet chocolate (50% to 64% cacao), such as Valrhona Equatoriale, Callebaut, or Ghirardelli, finely chopped

Directions:
1. Place the cream in a wide 2-quart saucepan and bring to a simmer over moderate heat.
2. Turn off the heat and instantly sprinkle the chocolate into the cream. Cover and allow to sit for 5 minutes. The heat of the cream should melt the chocolate. Softly mix the ganache until smooth. If the chocolate has not

melted completely, place over very low heat and mix frequently until melted, taking care not to burn it.
3. Let the glaze cool until warm, but not hot, and still fluid. (You may speed up the chilling process by stirring over an ice bath. If it becomes too firm, or if you would like to return it to a softer state, simply place over hot water or microwave briefly.)

Glaze Recipe 8: Peanut Butter Glaze

This glaze is for peanut butter lovers.
Yield: enough to coat the tops of about twenty-four 3-inch doughnuts
Ingredients:
- ½ cup chopped peanuts (unsalted or lightly salted)
- ⅔ to 1 cup whole milk
- 1 cup smooth peanut butter (such as Skippy; do not use natural)
- 4½ cups sifted confectioners' sugar

Directions:
1. Place the confectioners' sugar in a big container.
2. In a small saucepan, heat the peanut butter with ⅔ cup of the milk over medium-low heat until the mixture is hot but not simmering. Turn off the heat and gently whisk the peanut butter into the milk so that it begins to soften—it will not dissolve into the milk, which is okay.
3. Pour the milk and peanut butter over the confectioners' sugar and whisk rapidly until smooth. Put in the remaining ⅓ cup milk only if necessary to make a smooth, pourable glaze. Add mix in the peanuts. You can immerse the tops of your doughnuts directly in the glaze or spread it on top of the doughnuts using a small

offset spatula. If the glaze drips off the doughnuts too easily, simply cool it slightly before dipping.
4. Allow the glazed donut to sit until the glaze sets, about 5 minutes. Serve instantly.

Topping: Cinnamon-Sugar

The classis combination of cinnamon and sugar!
Yield: enough to coat the tops of about sixteen 3-inch doughnuts or about 24 doughnut holes or small fritters
Ingredients:
- 1 cup granulated sugar or superfine sugar
- 1½ teaspoons ground cinnamon

Directions:
1. Mix the sugar and cinnamon together in a shallow container big enough to hold a doughnut.
2. Place a still-warm doughnut on top of the mixture and toss around to coat well.

Frosting: Cream Cheese

Cream cheese is classic as it gets.
Yield: enough to coat the tops of about eighteen 2½-inch doughnuts
Ingredients:
- ½ cup (1 stick) unsalted butter, at room temperature, cut into pieces
- 1 8-ounce package cream cheese, at room temperature, cut into pieces
- 1 teaspoon pure vanilla extract
- 2 cups sifted confectioners' sugar

Directions:

1. Place all of the ingredients in a moderate-sized container and beat using an electric mixer until it begins to blend.
2. Scrape the container down once or twice and carry on beating until satiny smooth and creamy.

Filling: Pastry Cream

A classis smooth vanilla flavoured pastry cream. Can be stored in the fridge for about 2 days using an airtight container.
Yield: about 2½ cups, enough to fill about 40 doughnuts
Ingredients:
- ½ cup plus 2 tablespoons sugar
- 1 teaspoon pure vanilla extract
- 2 cups whole milk
- 2 large egg yolks, at room temperature
- 2 large eggs, at room temperature
- 2 tablespoons cornstarch
- 2 tablespoons unsalted butter, at room temperature, cut into pieces
- Pinch of salt

Directions:
1. Bring the milk to a boil in a moderate-sized nonreactive saucepan over moderate heat; turn off the heat and cover to keep warm.
2. Mix together the whole eggs, egg yolks, and sugar in a moderate-sized container until creamy. Mix in the cornstarch and salt until smooth.
3. Pour about one quarter of the warm milk over the egg mixture, whisking gently. Put in the remaining milk and whisk to combine. Instantly pour the mixture back into the pot and cook over medium to heat. Whisk almost continuously and watch for bubbles. As soon as the mixture comes to a boil, whisk rapidly and continuously

for 1 to 2 minutes. The pastry cream is ready when it is thick enough to mound when dropped from a spoon but still satiny.
4. Turn off the heat and whisk in the butter and vanilla. Allow the pastry cream to cool; mix intermittently to release the heat. When almost at room temperature, scrape into an airtight container, press plastic wrap directly against the surface (to keep a skin from forming), cover, and refrigerate for minimum 4 hours or until thoroughly chilled before using.

Advanced Donut Recipes

Now that you've mastered the art of making basic donuts and glazes, it is time to REALLY sink our teeth into making advanced donuts.
Many of the ingredients in the recipes that follow are basic recipes of the precious section, so be sure to keep looking back when you have to!
Let's do this!

Appamon Donuts

Cinnamon and apples go great on donuts!
Yield: 18 Donuts
Total Time to Prepare: 35 Minutes
Ingredients for the donuts:
- ¼ cup of butter, unsalted and melted
- ¼ cup of canola oil
- ¼ tsp. of baker's style baking soda
- ½ tsp. of salt

- ¾ cup of sugar, granulated
- 1 ½ tsp. of baker's style baking powder
- 1 cup of buttermilk
- 2 2/3 cup flour, all-purpose
- 2 eggs, large
- 2 granny smith apples, peeled and shredded
- 2 tsp. of cinnamon
- 2 tsp. of pure vanilla

Ingredients for the glaze:
- 1 cup of brown sugar, light and packed
- ½ cup of milk, whole
- 1 tbsp. of butter
- 1 ¼ cup of sugar, powdered
- ½ cup of walnuts, chopped and optional

Directions:
1. Preheat the oven to 425 degrees. As the oven heats up grease a big donut pan using cooking spray.
2. Use a big container and put in the butter, canola oil, large eggs, pure vanilla, buttermilk and granulated sugar. Stir thoroughly until well blended.
3. Then put in the all-purpose flour, baker's style baking powder and soda, dash of salt and ground cinnamon. Stir to blend.
4. Put in the shredded apples and stir until incorporated.
5. Pour the batter in the donut pan, making sure to fill each donut cup ¾ of the way full.
6. Put inside the oven to bake for 10 mins or until the donuts are thoroughly baked. Take out of the oven and move to a wire rack to cool completely.
7. As the donuts cool, make the glaze. To do this place a medium saucepan over moderate heat. Put in the brown sugar and whole milk. Bring this mixture to a boil. Allow to boil for 5 minutes and then turn off the

heat. Put in the butter and stir thoroughly until fully melted.
8. Put in the powdered sugar and whisk until a smooth consistency is achieved.
9. Immerse each of the tops of the donuts into the glaze. Place onto a wire rack to set. Sprinkle the walnuts over the top if using and serve.

Appy Donuts

Cinnamon and sugar make this donut insanely delicious and irresistible.

Yield: 22 Donuts
Total Time to Prepare: 20 Minutes
Ingredients for the donuts:
- ¼ cup of butter, unsalted, melted and cooled slightly
- ¼ tsp. of nutmeg
- ½ cup of buttermilk
- ½ tsp. of baker's style baking soda
- 1 ½ cup of apples, fresh, peeled and grated
- 1 ½ tbsp. of cinnamon
- 1 ½ tsp. of salt
- 1 cup of applesauce, unsweetened
- 1 cup of sugar
- 2 eggs, large
- 4 cups of flour, all-purpose
- 4 tsp. of baker's style baking powder

Ingredients for the coating:
- 1 cup of sugar
- 1 tbsp. of cinnamon, ground
- Butter, melted
- Dash of nutmeg, optional

Directions:
1. Preheat the oven to 375 degrees.

2. Use a big container and put in the all-purpose flour, baker's style baking powder and soda, dash of salt, ground cinnamon and dash of nutmeg. Stir thoroughly until well blended.
3. Use a different big container and put in the melted butter, large eggs, sugar, buttermilk and unsweetened applesauce. Stir thoroughly until well blended and pour this mixture into the flour mixture. Stir thoroughly until just blended.
4. Pour the donut batter into a large piping bag. Pipe the batter into each of the donut cups, making sure to fill ¾ of the way full.
5. Put inside the oven to bake for 12 to 15 minutes or until baked through. Remove and save for later to cool.
6. As the donuts cool add the cinnamon, nutmeg and sugar into a medium bowl. Stir thoroughly until well blended.
7. Brush the cooled donuts with the melted butter. Immerse the donuts in the cinnamon mixture. Serve.

Appy Fritters

Enjoy these as soon as they are made!

Yield: about ten 3-inch fritters

Ingredients:

Donuts:
- ⅔ cup whole milk
- 1 tablespoon baking powder
- 1 teaspoon finely grated lemon zest
- 1 teaspoon ground cinnamon
- 1 teaspoon salt
- 1½ tablespoons flavorless vegetable oil, such as canola, plus more for deep-frying
- 1½ tablespoons unsalted butter, melted

- 2 cups all-purpose flour
- 2 large eggs, at room temperature
- 2½ cups 1-inch chunks peeled and cored apples (from 1 large tart apple and 1 large sweet apple)
- 3 tablespoons firmly packed dark brown sugar

Cider syrup glaze:
- ½ a recipe [Cinnamon-Sugar Topping](#)
- ¾ teaspoon ground cinnamon
- 1½ cups sifted confectioners½ sugar
- 5 tablespoons cider syrup (see Field Notes)

Directions:
1. Mix together the flour, brown sugar, baking powder, cinnamon, and salt in a small container .
2. Mix together the eggs, milk, melted butter, 1½ tablespoons oil, and lemon zest in a big container. Fold in the dry mixture until a few streaks of flour remain. Softly fold in the apples until just combined.
3. Cover a rimmed baking sheet pan with a layer of three paper towels. Heat up 3 inches of oil using a deep pot or deep-fat fryer to 350° to 355°F. Once the oil has reached the desired temperature, use two large spoons to scoop up an amount of batter about the size of a tennis ball. Flatten the batter using the back of a spoon, and drop the newly formed disc into the oil. Fry multiple donuts simultaneously, without crowding. Fry until you see the donuts get a golden-brown colour, approximately 1 minute and 40 seconds, turn the donuts over, and fry for approximately 1 minute and 40 seconds more, until you see the donuts get the golden-brown colour on the other side too. With the help of a slotted spoon, remove each fritter from the oil and drain well using paper towels. Repeat with the remaining batter.

4. **For the glaze:** In a moderate sized saucepan set over low heat, heat the cider syrup only until warm. Mix in the confectioners' sugar and cinnamon until totally smooth. Using a teaspoon, drizzle the glaze over half of the batch of fritters (still resting on paper towels) while they are still warm; allow to sit for approximately 5 minutes to let the glaze set. Roll the remaining half of the batch in the cinnamon-sugar topping, coating all sides.

Banana Overload Donuts

This is a banana flavoured donut with a banana flavoured glaze. This is for all those banana lovers out there!

Yield: about ten 3-inch doughnuts

Ingredients:

Donuts:
- ¼ teaspoon freshly grated nutmeg
- ½ cup firmly packed light brown sugar
- ½ cup full-fat sour cream, at room temperature
- ½ cup lightly mashed very ripe banana
- ½ cup sifted cake flour
- ½ teaspoon baking soda
- ½ teaspoon salt
- 1 teaspoon pure vanilla extract
- 2 cups all-purpose flour
- 2 large eggs, at room temperature
- 2½ teaspoons baking powder
- Flavorless vegetable oil for deep-frying, such as canola

Banana glaze:
- ½ cup lightly mashed very ripe banana
- 2 teaspoons freshly squeezed lemon juice
- 1 cup sifted confectioners' sugar

Directions:
1. For the doughnuts: Mix together both flours, the baking powder, baking soda, salt, and nutmeg in a moderate-sized container .
2. Beat the brown sugar and eggs together in a big container using an electric mixer until pale and creamy, or mix thoroughly using your hands. Put in and mix in the mashed banana, sour cream, and vanilla just until well blended. Put in the dry mixture in two batches and mix using a wooden spoon only until the dough comes together. Cover and place in the fridge for minimum 2 hours or up to overnight.
3. Take the dough out of the fridge. Cover a rimmed baking sheet pan with a layer of three paper towels. Heat up 3 inches of oil using a deep pot or deep-fat fryer to 350° to 355°F.
4. As the oil heats, dust the work surface generously with flour. Place the dough on the readied surface (it will be very soft), coat the top of the dough slightly with flour, and roll the dough until it is ½ inch thick. Cut out donuts using a slightly floured 3-inch round cutter. Slowly gather all the left-over dough, press it together, roll the dough again to the same thickness, and cut out as many additional donuts as you possibly can.
5. Fry multiple donuts simultaneously, without crowding. Fry until your donuts become slightly golden brown, approximately 1½ minutes, turn the donuts over, and fry for approximately 1½ minutes more, until the other side looks slightly golden-brown too. With the help of a slotted spoon, take each donut out of the fryer and drain well using paper towels. Repeat the process for the rest of the donuts.
6. For the glaze: Mix together the mashed banana and lemon juice in a moderate-sized container until well

blended; there will still be some small bits of banana. Mix in the confectioners' sugar until the glaze is combined and fluid.
7. While the doughnuts are still somewhat warm, immerse the tops in the glaze and allow to sit for approximately 5 minutes to let the glaze set.

Beignets

These soft sweet rectangular treats will satisfy your sweet tooth!

Yield: about 20 beignets

Ingredients:

- ⅔ cup warm water (110° to 115°F)
- 3 tablespoons vegetable shortening
- ½ whole milk
- ¼ cup granulated sugar
- 1 large egg, at room temperature, beaten
- ½ teaspoon salt
- 3¼ to 3½ cups all-purpose flour
- Flavorless vegetable oil for deep-frying, such as canola
- Confectioners' sugar
- 1 0.25-ounce package active dry yeast

Directions:

1. Place the warm water in a big container and sprinkle the yeast over it. Stir to combine and allow to sit for 5 minutes.
2. Melt the shortening with the milk in a microwave or a small saucepan on the stovetop, then cool to lukewarm (110° to 115°F). Put in the shortening mixture, granulated sugar, egg, salt, and 2½ cups of the flour to the yeast mixture and mix using a wooden spoon or silicone spatula until well blended and smooth. The

mixture will have some body but will still be very wet and loose. Add mix in another 1 cup of the flour until the mixture becomes a slightly sticky, elastic dough, adding the remaining ¼ cup flour only if needed. Knead thoroughly by beating rapidly using a the spoon or spatula or use a stand mixer with the flat paddle or dough hook attachment. The mixture should be elastic, yet slightly sticky and not dry.
3. Put the dough in a buttered container, leaving plenty of headroom. Cover the container using plastic wrap and place in warm, draft-free location to rise until twice its initial size, approximately 1 hour.
4. Thoroughly flour two rimmed baking sheet pans. Softly punch down the dough. On a slightly floured work surface, roll out a large rectangle of dough ½ inch thick. Cut the dough with a pizza wheel into 3 × 2-inch rectangles. Place the rectangles, well spaced, on the prepared pans. Allow to rise in a warm, draft-free location until twice its initial size, approximately half an hour.
5. Coat two rimmed baking sheet pans with a layer of three paper towels. Heat up 3 inches of oil using a deep pot or deep-fat fryer to 350° to 355°F. Once the oil has reached the desired temperature, fry a few beignets at a time; do not crowd. Fry until your donuts become slightly golden brown, approximately 1 minute, turn the donuts over, and fry for approximately 1 minute more, until the other side looks slightly golden-brown too. With the help of a slotted spoon, remove each beignet from the oil and drain well using paper towels. Repeat with the remaining beignets.
6. While still warm, toss the beignets in a container of confectioners' sugar, arrange on a platter, then sprinkle with more confectioners' sugar.

Blueberry Creamy Fritters

A sweet, tender, and rich fritter tastes even better when filled with blueberries!

Yield: about 24 golf ball-size fritters

Ingredients:

Toppings:
- ½ a recipe <u>Cinnamon-Sugar Topping</u>
- ½ cup sifted confectioners' sugar
- 1 teaspoon ground cinnamon

Fritters:
- ½ teaspoon baking powder
- ½ teaspoon baking soda
- ½ teaspoon ground cinnamon
- ½ teaspoon salt
- ¾ cup fresh or frozen (thawed and drained) blueberries
- ¾ cup full-fat sour cream
- ¾ cup granulated sugar
- 1 cup all-purpose flour
- 1 cup sifted cake flour
- 1 large egg, at room temperature
- 1½ teaspoons pure vanilla extract
- Flavorless vegetable oil for deep-frying, such as canola

Directions:

1. For the toppings: Place the cinnamon-sugar topping in a small container. Stir together the confectioners' sugar and cinnamon in another small container.
2. For the fritters: Mix together both flours, the baking powder, baking soda, cinnamon, and salt in a big container . Mix together the sour cream, granulated sugar, egg, and vanilla in a moderate-sized container

until smooth. Put in the wet ingredients to the dry mixture and whisk gently until smooth.
3. Cover a rimmed baking sheet pan with a layer of three paper towels. Heat up 3 inches of oil using a deep pot or deep-fat fryer to 350° to 355°F. Once the oil has reached the desired temperature, use a 1 9/16-inch ice cream scoop to drop the batter (carefully) into the oil. Alternatively, you can make small rounds by scooping up the batter with one tablespoon and scraping it off into the oil with another tablespoon. Fry a few fritters at a time; do not crowd. Fry until you see the donuts get a golden-brown colour, approximately 1 minute and 10 seconds, turn the donuts over, and fry for approximately 1 minute and 10 seconds more, until you see the donuts get the golden-brown colour on the other side too. With the help of a slotted spoon, remove each fritter from the oil and drain well using paper towels. Repeat with the remaining batter.
4. While the donuts are still warm, roll half of the fritters in the granulated sugar-cinnamon mixture and half of the batch in the confectioners' sugar-cinnamon mixture.

Brown Bonanza Donuts

This donut tastes like a toffee, and the kids love it!
Yield: about twelve 3-inch doughnuts
Ingredients:
Donuts:
- ½ teaspoon baking soda
- ½ teaspoon freshly grated nutmeg
- 1 cup firmly packed dark brown sugar
- 1 cup full-fat sour cream, at room temperature
- 1 cup sifted cake flour
- 1 tablespoon baking powder

- 1 teaspoon salt
- 1½ teaspoons pure vanilla extract
- 2 large eggs, at room temperature
- 2½ cups all-purpose flour
- 7 tablespoons unsalted butter
- Flavorless vegetable oil for deep-frying, such as canola

Browned butter frosting:
- ½ cup (1 stick) unsalted butter, at room temperature
- 1 cup sifted confectioners' sugar
- Pinch of salt, or to taste

Directions:

1. For the doughnuts: Melt the butter in a small saucepan over moderate heat until it turns deep amber brown; don't allow it to burn. Measure out 5 tablespoons, which you'll need for the recipe; set aside. (If you have any left over, save for another purpose.)
2. Mix together both flours, the baking powder, salt, and baking soda in a moderate-sized container .
3. In a big container, blend the brown sugar and eggs using an electric mixer until pale and creamy, or mix thoroughly using your hands. Put in and mix in the reserved browned butter, vanilla, sour cream, and nutmeg until well blended. Put in the dry mixture in two batches and mix using a wooden spoon only until the dough comes together. Refrigerate for minimum 2 hours or up to overnight.
4. Take the dough out of the fridge. Cover a rimmed baking sheet pan with a layer of three paper towels. Heat up 3 inches of oil using a deep pot or deep-fat fryer to 350° to 355°F.
5. As the oil heats, lightly cover the work surface with flour. Place the dough on the readied surface, coat the top of the dough slightly with flour, and roll the dough until it is ½ inch thick. Cut out donuts using a slightly

floured 3-inch round cutter. Slowly gather all the leftover dough, press it together, roll the dough again to the same thickness, and cut out as many additional donuts as you possibly can.
6. Fry multiple donuts simultaneously, without crowding. Fry until your donuts become slightly golden brown, should take around 75 seconds, turn the donuts over, and fry for around 75 seconds once again, until the other side looks slightly golden-brown too. With the help of a slotted spoon, take each donut out of the fryer and drain well using paper towels. Repeat the process with the rest of the dough.
7. For the frosting: Melt the butter in a small saucepan over moderate heat until it turns deep amber brown; don't allow it to burn. Place the confectioners' sugar in a moderate-sized container. Mix in the browned butter until the glaze is perfectly smooth. Put in a pinch of salt, taste, and adjust as you wish. Drizzle the frosting over the cooled doughnuts using a parchment paper cone, fork, or spoon.

Buttercream-Filled Donuts

Yield: about twenty-six 2½-inch filled doughnuts

Ingredients:
- ¼ to ½ cup whole milk, at room temperature
- ¾ cup (1½ sticks) unsalted butter, at room temperature, cut into pieces
- 1 plump, moist vanilla bean
- 1 recipe Crispy Cream Donuts or Fundamental Yeast-Raised Donuts, prepared up to the first rise
- 1 teaspoon pure vanilla extract
- 6 ⅔ cups sifted confectioners' sugar

- Buttercream:
- Confectioners' sugar
- Pastry bag and coupler fitted with a Bismarck #230 tip

Directions:

1. Thoroughly flour two rimmed baking sheet pans. Softly punch down the dough and split it in half. Roll one piece of dough on a slightly floured work surface to ½-inch thickness. Cut out doughnuts with a slightly floured 2½-inch round cutter. Repeat the process with the rest of the dough. Slowly gather all the left-over dough, press it together, roll the dough again to the same thickness, and cut out as many additional donuts as you possibly can. Place doughnuts, well spaced, on the prepared pans. Allow to rise in a warm, draft-free location until twice its initial size, approximately half an hour.

2. While the doughnuts are rising, prepare the buttercream. In a big container, beat the butter using an electric mixer on medium-high speed until creamy, approximately 2 minutes . Put in 1 cup of the confectioners' sugar and the vanilla extract and beat until light and fluffy, about 3 minutes, scraping down the sides of the container once or twice. Slit the vanilla bean lengthwise and use a butter knife or teaspoon to scrape all of the tiny seeds into the frosting. Beat again to begin incorporating the seeds. Put in the remaining 5 ⅔ cups confectioners' sugar and ¼ cup of the milk, beating on high speed until the buttercream is silky smooth. The frosting should be soft enough so that it will flow easily through the piping tip. Keep thinning out with additional milk, one teaspoon at a time, if necessary to achieve this soft texture.

3. Coat two rimmed baking sheet pans with a layer of three paper towels. Heat up 3 inches of oil using a deep pot or deep-fat fryer to 350° to 355°F. Once the oil has

reached the desired temperature, fry a few doughnuts at a time; do not crowd. Fry until your donuts become slightly golden brown, approximately 1½ minutes, turn the donuts over, and fry for approximately 1½ minutes more, until the other side looks slightly golden-brown too. With the help of a slotted spoon, take each donut out of the fryer and drain well using paper towels. Repeat the process for the rest of the donuts. Cool until just barely warm to the touch.
4. Put the buttercream into the pastry bag. Insert the tip into the side of a doughnut. Squeeze the pastry bag and fill the doughnut with buttercream only until the center of the doughnut slightly bulges. (You are aiming to pipe a generous 2 to 3 teaspoons of filling inside.) Repeat the process for the rest of the donuts and pastry cream.
5. Toss the filled doughnuts in confectioners' sugar to coat completely.

Caracanbon Donuts

This donut is loaded with the goodness of caramel, pecan, and bourbon!

Yield: depends on doughnut recipe chosen; glaze recipe makes enough to coat twenty-four 3-inch doughnuts

Ingredients:
- 1 recipe [Sour Cream Donuts](#), [Traditional Buttermilk Donuts](#), or [Choco-Cake Donuts](#), cut into 3-inch rings, fried, and beginning to cool

Caramel-Bourbon-Pecan Glaze:
- ⅔ cup water
- 1½ cups heavy cream, at room temperature
- 1½ teaspoons pure vanilla extract
- 2¼ cups sugar

- 3 tablespoons bourbon
- 3 tablespoons unsalted butter, at room temperature
- Heaping ¼ teaspoon salt
- Scant 1 cup pecan halves, toasted and finely chopped

Directions:
1. Mix the sugar and water together in a deep pot (you need headroom, as it will bubble up furiously when the cream is added). Bring to a simmer on moderate-high heat, swirling the pan once or twice, but do not stir. Cook until the sugar is caramelized and has turned a dark golden brown. Turn off the heat and put in the cream; the mixture will bubble vigorously. After the bubbling subsides, place the pan back on the burner over low heat. Put in the butter and bourbon and whisk only until smooth. Turn off the heat and whisk in the vanilla, salt, and nuts. Pour the glaze into a heatproof container and cool until slightly thickened.
2. Coat two rimmed baking sheet pans using aluminium foil or parchment paper. Immerse the tops of the doughnuts into the glaze or spread it on top using a small offset spatula. Allow the glazed donut to sit on the readied pans until the glaze sets, 5 to 10 minutes.

Carrot Cake Donuts

A donut with the goodness of carrot, spices, and brown sugar topped with cream cheese frosting.
Yield: about sixteen 3-inch doughnuts
Ingredients:
- ¼ cup (½ stick) unsalted butter, melted and cooled
- ¼ cup walnut halves, finely chopped
- ½ cup dark raisins, chopped
- ½ cup sifted cake flour
- ½ teaspoon freshly grated nutmeg

- ½ teaspoon salt
- 1 cup finely shredded raw carrots
- 1 cup firmly packed light brown sugar
- 1 cup mashed cooked carrots (Peel and thinly slice 4 large carrots, cover with water, boil until soft, drain, then process until smooth in a food processor fitted with a metal blade)
- 1 recipe [Cream Cheese Frosting](#)
- 1 tablespoon plus 1 teaspoon baking powder
- 1 teaspoon baking soda
- 1½ teaspoons ground cinnamon
- 2 large eggs, at room temperature
- 2 tablespoons flavorless vegetable oil, such as canola, plus more for deep-frying
- 3 cups all-purpose flour

Directions:

1. Mix together both flours, the baking powder, cinnamon, baking soda, nutmeg, and salt in a moderate-sized container. Toss in the raisins and nuts.
2. In a big container, blend the brown sugar and eggs using an electric mixer until pale and creamy, or mix thoroughly using your hands. Put in and mix in the cooked carrots, shredded carrots, melted butter, and 2 tablespoons oil until well blended. Put in the dry mixture in two batches and mix using a wooden spoon only until the dough comes together. Cover and place in the fridge for minimum 1 hour or up to overnight.
3. Take the dough out of the fridge. Cover a rimmed baking sheet pan with a layer of three paper towels; set aside. Prepare a deep pot or deep-fat fryer. Heat 3 inches of oil to 350° to 355°F.
4. As the oil heats, dust the work surface generously with flour. Place the dough on the readied surface, coat the top of the dough slightly with flour, and roll the dough

until it is ½ inch thick. Cut out donuts using a slightly floured 3-inch round cutter. Slowly gather all the leftover dough, press it together, roll the dough again to the same thickness, and cut out as many additional donuts as you possibly can.
5. Fry multiple donuts simultaneously, without crowding. Fry until your donuts become slightly golden brown, approximately 1½ minutes, turn the donuts over, and fry for approximately 1½ minutes more, until the other side looks slightly golden-brown too. With the help of a slotted spoon, take each donut out of the fryer and drain well using paper towels. Repeat the process for the rest of the donuts.
6. While the doughnuts are still barely warm, spread the tops with the frosting using a small offset spatula.

Cheesecake Loaded Donuts

These delicious donuts have a cheesecake filling!
Yield: about twenty-six 2½-inch filled doughnuts
Ingredients:
- 1 recipe Crispy Cream Donuts or Fundamental Yeast-Raised Donuts, cut into 2½-inch rounds, fried, and beginning to cool
- Sifted confectioners' sugar

Cheesecake filling:
- ¼ cup granulated sugar
- ¼ teaspoon pure vanilla extract
- 1 8-ounce package cream cheese, at room temperature, cut into pieces
- 1 cup heavy cream, plus more as needed
- 1 teaspoon freshly squeezed lemon juice
- Pastry bag and coupler fitted with a Bismarck #230 tip

Directions:
1. While they are still somewhat warm, roll the doughnuts on all sides in the confectioners' sugar. Allow the donuts to cool on clean racks.
2. For the cheesecake filling: In a moderate-sized container, beat the cream cheese using an electric mixer until very smooth and creamy. Put in the cream and beat on high speed until well blended and smooth. The cream will thicken and the entire mixture will have a thick consistency. Put in the granulated sugar and beat until it dissolves and the mixture is thick and has a smooth, creamy body. Put in and mix in the lemon juice and vanilla. The mixture should be the right consistency to be able to be piped through a pastry tip. If it is too thick, beat in more cream, 1 teaspoon at a time.
3. Fill the pastry bag with the cheesecake filling. Insert the tip into the side of a cooled doughnut. Squeeze the pastry bag and fill the doughnut with pastry cream only until the center of the doughnut slightly bulges. (You are aiming to pipe a generous 2 to 3 teaspoons of filling inside.) Repeat the process for the rest of the donuts and filling.

Choco Blast Donuts

This is the donut you make when you're craving some chocolate.

Yield: 8 Donuts
Total Time to Prepare: 25 Minutes
Ingredients for the donuts:
- ¼ cup of brown sugar, light and packed
- ¼ tsp. of salt
- ½ tsp. of baker's style baking soda
- ¾ cup of flour, all-purpose

- 1 ½ tsp. of pure vanilla
- 1 egg, large
- 1/3 cup of cocoa
- 2 ½ tbsp. of butter, melted and cooled
- 2/3 cup of buttermilk
- 3 tbsp. of sugar, granulated

Ingredients for the glaze:

- ¾ cup of icing sugar
- 2 tsp. of corn syrup
- 3 tbsp. of cocoa
- 3 to 4 tbsp. of cream
- Rainbow sprinkles, optional

Directions:

1. Preheat the oven to 350 degrees. As the oven heats up grease a big donut pan using cooking spray.
2. Use a moderate sized container and put in the all-purpose flour, cocoa, baker's style baking soda and dash of salt. Stir thoroughly until well blended.
3. Use a different moderate sized container and put in the melted butter, large egg, light brown sugar, granulated sugar, pure vanilla and buttermilk. Whisk until uniformly mixed.
4. Add the wet ingredients to the flour mixture. Stir thoroughly until a thick batter forms.
5. Pour the batter into the greased donut pan.
6. Put inside the oven to bake for 10 mins or until the donuts are thoroughly baked. Remove and save for later on a wire rack to cool.
7. While the cakes are cooling, make the glaze. To do this use a moderate sized container and put in the icing sugar, cocoa, cream and corn syrup. Whisk until a smooth consistency is achieved.
8. Once the donuts are cooled, dip the tops of the donuts into the glaze. Sprinkle the rainbow sprinkles over the

top and save for later to rest for 5 minutes or until the glaze is set. Serve.

Choco-Coated Strawberry Donuts

Yield: about twenty-four 2½-inch filled doughnuts

Ingredients:
- 1 2-ounce package (about 2 cups) freeze-dried strawberries (optional)
- 1 recipe Yeast-Raised Choco Donuts, prepared through the first rise
- 1½ cups strawberry preserves
- 1½ recipes Dark Chocolate Ganache Glaze
- Flavorless vegetable oil for deep-frying, such as canola

Directions:
1. Thoroughly flour two rimmed baking sheet pans. Softly punch down the dough and split it in half. Roll one piece of dough on a slightly floured work surface to ¼-inch thickness. Cut out dough rounds with a slightly floured 2½-inch round cutter. Repeat the process with the rest of the dough. Slowly gather all the left-over dough, press it together, roll out the dough, and cut out as many additional rounds as possible. Make sure you end up with an even number.
2. Using two cereal spoons, dollop about 2 teaspoons of strawberry preserves in the centers of half of the dough rounds. Immerse a pastry brush in room-temperature water and lightly brush the edges of the dough around the preserves. Place a plain round on top of each filled round and press the edges together with your fingertips to seal them well.
3. Place the doughnuts, well spaced, on the prepared pans. Allow to rise in a warm, draft-free location until twice its initial size, approximately half an hour.

4. Cover a rimmed baking sheet pan with a layer of three paper towels. Heat up 3 inches of oil using a deep pot or deep-fat fryer to 350° to 355°F. Once the oil has reached the desired temperature, fry a few doughnuts at a time; do not crowd. Fry until your donuts become slightly golden brown, approximately 1½ minutes, turn the donuts over, and fry for approximately 1½ minutes more, until the other side looks slightly golden-brown too. With the help of a slotted spoon, take each donut out of the fryer and drain well using paper towels. Repeat the process for the rest of the donuts.
5. While the doughnuts are still warm, immerse the tops in the glaze and place a few slices of freeze-dried strawberries, if using, on top of the glaze while it is still wet. Allow to sit for approximately 5 minutes to allow the ganache to set.

Choco-Frosted Donuts

Kids absolutely love this recipe!

Yield: 12 Donuts

Total Time to Prepare: 20 Minutes

Ingredients for the donuts:
- ¼ tsp. of cinnamon
- ¼ tsp. of lemon juice, fresh
- ¼ tsp. of nutmeg
- ¼ tsp. of pure vanilla
- ½ tsp. of salt
- ¾ cup of buttermilk
- ¾ cup of sugar
- 1 ½ tsp. of baker's style baking powder
- 1 cup of dark chocolate, melted
- 2 cups of flour, all-purpose

- 2 cups of sugar, powdered
- 2 eggs, large and beaten
- 2 tbsp. of butter, melted
- 3 tbsp. of milk, whole
- Ingredients for the chocolate glaze:
- Ingredients for the white glaze:

Directions:

1. Preheat the oven to 425 degrees. As the oven heats up grease two big donut pans using cooking spray.
2. Take a large container and put in the all-purpose flour, sugar, baking powder, nutmeg, ground cinnamon and dash of salt. Stir thoroughly until uniformly mixed.
3. Put in the buttermilk, fresh lemon juice, large eggs and melted butter. Stir thoroughly until just mixture.
4. Pour the batter into the donut pan, making sure to fill each donut cup ¾ of the way full.
5. Put inside the oven to bake for 10 mins or until the donuts are thoroughly baked. Take out of the oven and move to a wire rack to cool completely.
6. As the donuts cool make the white and chocolate glaze. To do this add all of the ingredients for the white glaze into a little container. Whisk until a smooth consistency is achieved. In a different little container melt the dark chocolate until a smooth consistency is achieved.
7. Immerse the top side of the donuts into the white glaze first and then in the melted chocolate. Place back onto the wire rack to sit for 5 minutes or until the glaze is set.

Choco-Glazed Donut

Another donut to quench chocolate cravings!
Yield: 10 to 12 Donuts
Total Time to Prepare: 30 Minutes
Ingredients for the donuts:

- ¼ cup of brown sugar, light and packed
- ¼ cup of cocoa, powdered
- ¼ cup of sugar, granulated
- ¼ tsp. of salt
- ½ cup of milk, whole
- ¾ cup of flour, all-purpose
- 1 egg, large
- 1 tsp. of baker's style baking powder
- 1 tsp. of pure vanilla
- 2 tbsp. of vegetable oil

Ingredients for the frosting:

- ¾ cup of chocolate chips, semi-sweet
- 1 tbsp. of honey
- 3 tbsp. of butter, cut into small squares

Directions:

1. Start by greasing a big donut pan using cooking spray. Set aside and heat up the oven to 350 degrees.
2. Use a moderate sized container and put in the all-purpose flour, light brown sugar, granulated sugar, powdered cocoa, baker's style baking powder and dash of salt. Stir thoroughly until blended.
3. In a different big container put in the whole milk, large egg, canola oil and pure vanilla. Stir to mix and pour into the flour mixture. Stir once more until just blended.
4. Pour the donut batter into a large piping bag. Pipe the dough into the prepared donut pan, making sure to fill each donut cup at least ¾ of the way full.
5. Put inside the oven to bake for 10 to 12 minutes at 350 degrees or until golden brown. Take out of the oven and move to a wire rack to cool completely.
6. As the donuts cool, make the frosting. To do this place a double boiler over moderate heat. Put in the butter, chocolate chips and honey. Stir thoroughly until melted.

7. Immerse the tops of the donuts into the ganache. Set aside to set for 15 to 20 minutes before serving.

Chocolate Mousse Donuts

Delicious fluffy donuts filled with chocolate mousse!
Yield: about twenty-eight 2½-inch filled doughnuts
Ingredients:
- 1 recipe Crispy Cream Donuts or Fundamental Yeast-Raised Donuts, cut into 2½-inch rounds, fried, and cooled
- 2 recipes Cocoa Glaze or Dark Chocolate Glaze
- Pastry bag and coupler fitted with a Bismarck #230 tip

Chocolate mousse:
- ⅛ teaspoon pure vanilla extract
- ¼ cup heavy cream, chilled
- 1 large egg, separated
- 1 tablespoon sugar
- 1 tablespoon unsalted butter
- 2 ounces semisweet or bittersweet chocolate (not more than 60% cacao), such as Callebaut or Ghirardelli, finely chopped
- Pinch of cream of tartar

Directions:
1. For the mousse: Melt the chocolate and butter together in a microwave or the top of a double boiler over simmering water; mix until smooth. Turn off the heat and cool slightly. Scrape the mixture into a moderate-sized container (or microwave it in a moderate-sized container to begin with). Mix in the egg yolk.
2. Whisk the egg white in a clean, grease-free container with a large balloon whisk until frothy; whisk in the cream of tartar until soft peaks form. Sprinkle the sugar over the top and whip until stiff peaks form. Fold about

half of the egg white into the chocolate mixture to lighten, then fold in the remainder until just a few streaks of white remain. Wash and dry the whisk well.
3. Mix together the cream and vanilla in a small container until soft peaks form. Fold the cream into the chocolate mousse until no streaks remain. Cover the container and refrigerate until firm, at least 4 hours or up to overnight.
4. Scrape the chilled mousse into the pastry bag. Insert the tip into the side of a cooled doughnut. Squeeze the pastry bag and fill the doughnut with mousse only until the center of the doughnut slightly bulges. (You are aiming to pipe a generous 2 to 3 teaspoons of filling inside.) Repeat the process for the rest of the donuts and mousse.
5. Immerse the tops of the doughnuts in the glaze and allow to sit for approximately 5 minutes to let the glaze set.

Chocomel Donuts

Delicious chocolate cake donuts dipped in a dark caramel glaze!
Yield: about fourteen 3-inch doughnuts
Ingredients:

- 1 6-ounce block bittersweet or semisweet chocolate, such as Valrhona Caraque, Caraïbe, Extra Bitter, or Equatoriale, or Callebaut

Caramel glaze:

- ½ cup water
- 1 cup heavy cream, at room temperature
- 1 recipe Choco-Cake Donuts, cut into 3-inch rings, fried, and beginning to cool
- 2 cups sugar
- Fleur de sel

Directions:
1. Use a sharp vegetable peeler to chip away small bits off the block of chocolate straight into an airtight plastic container. These may be made a few days ahead and placed in the fridge.
2. **For the glaze:** Mix the sugar and water in a deep moderate-sized saucepan. Stir over moderate heat until the sugar dissolves. Raise the heat and boil without stirring, intermittently brushing down the sides of the pan using a wet pastry brush. Watch cautiously for the moment when the sugar syrup just begins to exhibit color, should take around 5 to 10 minutes after it comes to a boil. Watch continuously at this point, as the color will develop rapidly, changing from pale gold to rich amber. Keep boiling and within a minute it will darken to a rich reddish brown, the color of a pecan. Instantly turn off the heat. Gradually pour the cream over the caramel. It will bubble up; just let it bubble and then subside. Stir slowly until smooth. If the caramel becomes hard, place the pan back over low heat and whisk gently until smooth. Pour the glaze into a heatproof container and cool until slightly thickened.
3. Coat two rimmed baking sheet pans using aluminium foil or parchment paper and coat with nonstick cooking spray.
4. While the doughnuts are still warm, immerse the tops in the glaze or spread it using a small offset spatula. Allow the donuts to sit on the readied pans until the glaze begins to cool. Sprinkle generously with dark chocolate curls while the glaze is cool but still a bit sticky. Sprinkle with a few grains of salt.

Choco-Peanut Butter Donuts

This one is a kids' favourite.

Yield: 18 Donuts

Total Time to Prepare: 30 Minutes

Ingredients for the donuts:

- ¼ tsp. of salt
- ½ cup of cocoa, unsweetened and powdered
- ¾ cup of sugar, granulated
- 1 cup of milk, whole
- 2 cups of flour, wheat
- 2 eggs, large
- 2 tsp. of baker's style baking powder
- 2 tsp. of pure vanilla
- 3 tbsp. of butter, unsalted and melted

Ingredients for the frosting:

- 1 cup of confectioner's sugar
- 2 tbsp. of butter, unsalted
- 3 tbsp. of peanut butter, creamy
- 3 to 4 tbsp. of heavy cream

Directions:

1. First preheat the oven to 350 degrees. Grease two big donut pans using cooking spray.
2. Use a moderate sized container and put in the wheat flour, powdered cocoa, baker's style baking powder and dash of salt. Stir thoroughly until well blended.
3. Use a different big container and put in the sugar and melted butter. Then put in the whole milk, large eggs and pure vanilla. Whisk until uniformly mixed. Add into the flour mixture and fold until just combined and moist.
4. Pour the batter into a piping bag. Grease donut pans and pipe the donut batter into the pans, filling 2/3 of the way full in every donut cup.

5. Put inside the oven to bake for 10 minutes or until thoroughly baked. Take out of the oven and move to a wire rack to cool for 5 to 10 minutes.
6. As the donuts cool, make the frosting. To do this add the creamy peanut butter and butter into a little container. Microwave for 30 seconds. Stir until uniformly mixed. Put in the sugar and whisk until a smooth consistency is achieved.
7. Immerse the tops of the donuts into the frosting and allow them to set. Serve.

Choco-Sour Cream Donuts

Rich and moist donuts with the goodness of chocolate.
Yield: about twelve 3-inch doughnuts
Ingredients:
- ⅓ cup sifted Dutch-processed cocoa powder
- ½ teaspoon baking soda
- 1 cup full-fat sour cream, at room temperature
- 1 cup plus 2 tablespoons sugar
- 1 cup sifted cake flour
- 1 tablespoon baking powder
- 1 teaspoon salt
- 1¾ cups all-purpose flour
- 2 large eggs, at room temperature
- 2 teaspoons pure vanilla extract
- 5 tablespoons unsalted butter, melted and cooled
- Flavorless vegetable oil for deep-frying, such as canola

Directions:
1. Mix together both flours, the cocoa, baking powder, baking soda, and salt in a moderate-sized container.
2. In a big container, blend the sugar and eggs using an electric mixer until pale and creamy, or mix thoroughly using your hands. Put in and mix in the sour cream,

melted butter, and vanilla until well blended. Put in the dry mixture in two batches and mix using a wooden spoon only until the dough comes together. Cover and place in the fridge for minimum 2 hours or up to overnight.
3. Take the dough out of the fridge. Cover a rimmed baking sheet pan with a layer of three paper towels. Heat up 3 inches of oil using a deep pot or deep-fat fryer to 350° to 355°F.
4. As the oil heats, dust a work surface with flour. Scrape the chilled dough onto the surface, coat the top of the dough slightly with flour, and roll the dough until it is ½ inch thick. Cut out donuts using a slightly floured 3-inch round cutter. Slowly gather all the left-over dough, press it together, roll the dough again to the same thickness, and cut out as many additional donuts as you possibly can.
5. Fry multiple donuts simultaneously, without crowding. Fry approximately 1½ minutes, turn the donuts over, and fry for approximately 1½ minutes more, until just cooked through. With the help of a slotted spoon, take each donut out of the fryer and drain well using paper towels. Repeat the process with the rest of the dough.

Choco-Spice Donuts

Chocolate with an awesome combination of spices!
Yield: about fourteen 3-inch doughnuts
Ingredients:
- 1 recipe Choco-Cake Donuts , made adding 1 teaspoon each ground cinnamon and freshly grated nutmeg and ½ teaspoon each ground cardamom, ground cloves, ground ginger, and cayenne pepper (optional) to the dry

mixture, cut into 3-inch rings, fried, and beginning to cool
- 1 recipe Cinnamon-Sugar Topping, prepared adding ½ teaspoon ground cardamom

Directions:
1. While they are still somewhat warm, roll the doughnuts on all sides in the cinnamon-sugar-cardamom topping.
2. Enjoy!

Choco-Toffee Donuts

Simple sour cream donuts with toffee bits and chocolate chips!
Yield: about twelve 3-inch doughnuts
Ingredients:
- ⅔ cup toffee bits
- 1 recipe Dark Chocolate Ganache Glaze
- 1 recipe Sour Cream Donuts, prepared folding 1 cup each miniature semisweet chocolate morsels and toffee bits (such as Heath Bits 'O Brickle) into the final dough, cut into 3-inch rings, fried, and beginning to cool

Directions:
1. While the doughnuts are still somewhat warm, immerse the tops in the glaze.
2. Sprinkle well with the toffee bits while the glaze is still wet.
3. Allow to sit for approximately 5 minutes to let the glaze set.

Churros Choco-dip

Churros are light, crisp, and very easy to make. They go great with chocolate dipping sauce!
Yield: about 36 churros

Ingredients:

Chocolate sauce:
- ⅛ teaspoon ground cinnamon
- ½ a recipe <u>Cinnamon-Sugar Topping</u>
- ½ teaspoon pure vanilla extract
- ½ teaspoon salt
- 1 cup all-purpose flour
- 1 cup water
- 1 tablespoon cornstarch
- 1 teaspoon sugar
- 2 cups whole milk
- 3 large eggs, at room temperature
- 4 ounces semisweet chocolate, such as Callebaut or Ghirardelli, finely chopped
- 6 tablespoons (¾ stick) unsalted butter, cut into pieces
- Churros:
- Flavorless vegetable oil for deep-frying, such as canola
- Pastry bag fitted with a large star tip (about ½-inch opening), such as Ateco #847

Directions:

1. For the chocolate sauce: Place the chocolate and 1 cup of the milk in a small, heavy saucepan over low heat. Cook, whisking frequently, until the chocolate is melted and smooth. In the meantime, whisk the remaining 1 cup milk with the cornstarch in a small container to dissolve the cornstarch, then whisk it into the hot chocolate mixture. Bring to a gentle boil, whisking continuously, and boil until the mixture has thickened, 1 to 2 minutes. Turn off the heat and keep warm.
2. For the churros: Mix the water, butter, sugar, and salt in a moderate-sized saucepan. Bring to a rolling boil on moderate-high heat and instantly turn off the heat. Rapidly mix in the flour all at once with a wooden spoon, until the dough comes together. Place over very

low heat and keep stirring to dry out the dough, approximately 1 minute. It should come away cleanly from the sides of the saucepan. Scrape it into the container of a stand mixer fitted with a paddle attachment. Turn on medium speed and put in the eggs one at a time, allowing each egg to be absorbed before continuing. Put in and mix in the vanilla and cinnamon. The batter should be smooth, golden yellow, and firm enough to hold a shape when mounded with a spoon.
3. Place the cinnamon-sugar topping in a shallow container. Coat two rimmed baking sheet pans with a layer of three paper towels. Scrape dough into pastry bag.
4. Heat up 3 inches of oil using a deep pot or deep-fat fryer to 350° to 355°F. Once the oil has reached the desired temperature, pipe 5-inch-long strips of dough directly into the hot oil, cutting the dough with a scissor or knife to release it from the tip. Fry multiple donuts simultaneously, without crowding. Fry until you see the donuts get a golden-brown colour, approximately 1 minute, flip over, and fry for approximately 1 minute more, until golden-brown on the other side. With the help of a slotted spoon, remove each churro from the oil, place on paper towels for a moment, then instantly roll in the cinnamon sugar, tossing to coat completely. Transfer to a serving plate and repeat with remaining dough.
5. As soon as all of the churros are fried and coated, serve instantly with the dipping sauce.

Cider-Buttermilk Donuts

A buttermilk donut with the goodness of apple cider!

Yield: about twenty-four 3-inch doughnuts
Ingredients:
- ½ teaspoon baking soda
- ½ teaspoon ground allspice
- ½ teaspoon salt
- ⅔ cup sugar
- 1 cup apple cider, at room temperature
- 1 cup sifted cake flour
- 1 recipe Cinnamon-Sugar Topping (if you want)
- 2 large eggs, at room temperature
- 2 teaspoons baking powder
- 2 teaspoons ground cinnamon
- 2½ cups all-purpose flour
- 6 tablespoons (¾ stick) unsalted butter, melted and cooled
- Flavorless vegetable oil for deep-frying, such as canola

Directions:
1. Mix together both flours, the baking powder, cinnamon, baking soda, salt, and allspice in a moderate-sized container .
2. In a big container, blend the sugar and eggs using an electric mixer until pale and creamy, or mix thoroughly using your hands. Put in and mix in the cider and melted butter until well blended. Put in the dry mixture in two batches and mix using a wooden spoon only until the dough comes together. Cover and place in the fridge for minimum 1 hour or up to overnight.
3. Cover a rimmed baking sheet pan with a layer of three paper towels. Heat up 3 inches of oil using a deep pot or deep-fat fryer to 350° to 355°F.
4. As the oil heats, lightly cover the work surface with flour. Place the dough on the readied surface, coat the top of the dough slightly with flour, and roll the dough until it is ½ inch thick. Cut out donuts using a slightly

floured 3-inch round cutter. Slowly gather all the leftover dough, press it together, roll the dough again to the same thickness, and cut out as many additional donuts as you possibly can. Place the cinnamon sugar, if using, in a shallow container.
5. Fry multiple donuts simultaneously, without crowding. Fry until your donuts become slightly golden brown, should take around 75 seconds, turn the donuts over, and fry for around 75 seconds once again, until the other side looks slightly golden-brown too. With the help of a slotted spoon, take each donut out of the fryer and drain well using paper towels.
6. If desired, instantly transfer the doughnuts to the container of cinnamon sugar and roll and toss them to coat completely. Repeat the process with the rest of the dough.

Classical Donuts

Coated with cinnamon and sugar, this donut tastes scrumptious!
Yield: 8 to 10 Donuts
Total Time to Prepare: 20 Minutes
Ingredients for the donuts:
- ¾ tsp. of cinnamon, ground
- ¾ tsp. of nutmeg, ground
- ¾ tsp. of salt
- 1 ½ cup of sugar, granulated
- 1 ½ cups of milk, whole
- 1 egg, large
- 3 ½ tbsp. of butter, soft
- 4 ½ tsp. of baker's style baking powder
- 6 cups of all-purpose flour

- Canola oil, for frying

Ingredients for the coating:
- 1 ½ tbsp. of cinnamon, ground
- 1 cup of sugar, granulated

Directions:
1. First put in the sugar and butter into a large bowl. Beat with an electric mixer until a smooth consistency is achieved. Put in the whole milk, large egg, all-purpose flour, baking powder, dash of salt, ground cinnamon and nutmeg. Stir thoroughly until well blended.
2. Roll out the donut dough on a slightly floured surface until ½ inch in thickness. Use a doughnut cutter and cut out even rounds.
3. Heat up a deep fat fryer with the canola oil until the oil reaches 375 degrees. Once the oil is hot enough drop in the doughnuts. Fry for 3 to 5 minutes or until golden on both sides. Take out of the oven and move to a plate lined with paper towels to drain.
4. While the donuts are frying add the granulated sugar and cinnamon for the coating into a little container. Stir thoroughly until blended.
5. Add the drained donuts to the cinnamon and sugar mixture. Toss well to coat and serve.

Coconut Overload Donuts

A yeast-raised donut filled with coconut pastry, and topped with coconut glaze!

Yield: about twenty-six 2½-inch filled doughnuts

Ingredients:
- 1 recipe Crispy Cream Donuts or Fundamental Yeast-Raised Donuts, prepared through the first rise
- Pastry bag and coupler fitted with a Bismarck #230 tip

Coconut pastry cream:

- ½ cup granulated sugar
- 1 tablespoon unsalted butter, at room temperature
- 1½ teaspoons pure vanilla extract
- 2 cups pure unsweetened coconut milk
- 2 large egg yolks
- 2 large eggs
- 3 tablespoons cornstarch
- Pinch of salt

Coconut glaze:
- ½ teaspoon pure vanilla extract
- ¾ cup pure unsweetened coconut milk
- 2 cups lightly packed sweetened long-shred coconut
- 4 cups sifted confectioner' sugar

Directions:

1. For the pastry cream: Bring the coconut milk to a boil in a moderate-sized nonreactive saucepan over moderate heat; turn off the heat and cover to keep warm.
2. In the meantime, whisk together the whole eggs, egg yolks, and granulated sugar in a moderate-sized container until creamy. Mix in the cornstarch and salt until smooth.
3. Pour about one-quarter of the warm coconut milk into the egg mixture, whisking gently. Put in the remaining milk and whisk to combine. Instantly pour the mixture back into the saucepan and cook over medium-low heat. Whisk almost continuously and watch for bubbles. As soon as the mixture begins to boil, whisk rapidly and continuously over the heat for 1 to 2 minutes. The pastry cream should be thick enough to mound when dropped from a spoon, but still be satiny. Turn off the heat and whisk in the butter and vanilla.
4. Let the pastry cream cool; mix intermittently to release the heat. When it is almost at room temperature, scrape it into an airtight container, press plastic wrap

directly onto the surface (to keep a skin from forming), snap on the lid, and refrigerate until thoroughly chilled, at least 4 hours or up to 3 days.

5. For the doughnuts: Thoroughly flour two rimmed baking sheet pans. Softly punch down the dough and split it in half. Roll one piece of dough on a slightly floured work surface to ½-inch thickness. Cut out doughnuts with a slightly floured 2½-inch round cutter. Repeat the process with the rest of the dough. Slowly gather all the left-over dough, press it together, roll the dough again to the same thickness, and cut out as many additional donuts as you possibly can.

6. Place the doughnuts, well spaced, on the prepared pans. Allow to rise in a warm, draft-free location until twice its initial size, approximately half an hour.

7. Coat two rimmed baking sheet pans with a layer of three paper towels. Heat up 3 inches of oil using a deep pot or deep-fat fryer to 350° to 355°F. Once the oil has reached the desired temperature, fry a few doughnuts at a time; do not crowd. Fry until your donuts become slightly golden brown, approximately 1½ minutes, turn the donuts over, and fry for approximately 1½ minutes more, until the other side looks slightly golden-brown too. With the help of a slotted spoon, take each donut out of the fryer and drain well using paper towels. Repeat the process for the rest of the donuts. Cool thoroughly.

8. Scrape the pastry cream into the pastry bag. Insert the tip into the side of a cooled doughnut. Squeeze the pastry bag and fill the doughnut with pastry cream only until the center of the doughnut slightly bulges. (You are aiming to pipe a generous 2 to 3 teaspoons of filling inside.) Repeat the process for the rest of the donuts and pastry cream.

9. For the glaze: Place the confectioners' sugar in a medium container. Mix in the coconut milk a little bit at a time until the desired consistency is reached. Mix in the vanilla. Immerse the top of each doughnut in the glaze. Sprinkle generously with shredded coconut while the glaze is still wet. Allow to sit for approximately 5 minutes to let the glaze set.

Coffee Blast Donuts

This one is for all the coffee lovers out there!
Yield: about twenty-four 2½-inch filled doughnuts
Ingredients:
Espresso cream filling:
- ½ cup sugar
- 1 teaspoon pure vanilla extract
- 2 cups whole milk, at room temperature
- 2 tablespoons instant espresso powder
- 2 tablespoons unsalted butter
- 5 large egg yolks, at room temperature
- 6 tablespoons all-purpose flour
- Pinch of salt

Donuts:
- 1 cup plus 2 tablespoons warm whole milk (110° to 115°F)
- 4 cups all-purpose flour
- ¼ cup sugar
- 1 teaspoon ground cinnamon
- ½ teaspoon salt
- 10 tablespoons (1¼ sticks) unsalted butter, melted and cooled to lukewarm
- 2 large eggs, at room temperature
- Flavorless vegetable oil for deep-frying, such as canola

- 1 0.25-ounce package active dry yeast

Topping:
- ½ cup sugar
- 2 teaspoons Dutch-processed cocoa powder
- 2 teaspoons ground cinnamon
- Pastry bag and coupler fitted with a Bismarck #230 tip

Directions:

1. For the filling: Mix together the sugar, flour, and espresso powder in a heavy moderate-sized saucepan. Gradually whisk in the milk until smooth, then whisk in the egg yolks and salt. Put in the butter. Cook on moderate-high heat until the mixture thickens and gently boils, whisking continuously, about 6 minutes. Mix in the vanilla. Transfer to a storage container. Press plastic wrap directly onto the surface (to keep a skin from forming). Chill until cold, at least 6 hours and up to 2 days.

2. For the doughnuts: Place the warm milk in a big container and sprinkle the yeast over it. Stir to combine and allow to sit for 5 minutes. Mix together the flour, sugar, cinnamon, and salt in a moderate-sized container . Mix together the melted butter and eggs in a separate container until well blended.

3. Whisk the egg mixture into the yeast mixture using your hands or use the dough hook of a stand mixer. Put in and mix in the flour mixture about ½ cup at a time, beating until the dough is smooth and beginning to pull away from the sides of the container, about 5 minutes. Scrape the dough from the hook, if using. Let the dough rest for 5 minutes. Put the dough in a buttered container (the dough will be sticky), leaving plenty of headroom. Cover the container using plastic wrap and refrigerate overnight.

4. Thoroughly flour two rimmed baking sheet pans. Softly punch down the dough and split it in half. Roll one piece of dough on a slightly floured work surface to ⅓-inch thickness. Cut out doughnuts with a slightly floured 2½-inch round cutter. Repeat the process with the rest of the dough. Slowly gather all the left-over dough, press it together, roll the dough again to the same thickness, and cut out as many additional donuts as you possibly can.
5. Place the doughnuts, well spaced, on the prepared pans. Allow to rise in a warm, draft-free location until twice its initial size, approximately 1 hour.
6. Coat two rimmed baking sheet pans with a layer of three paper towels. Heat up 3 inches of oil using a deep pot or deep-fat fryer to 350° to 355°F.
7. As the oil heats, make the topping by whisking together the sugar, cocoa, and cinnamon in a wide shallow container.
8. Fry multiple donuts simultaneously, without crowding. Fry until your donuts become slightly golden brown, should take around 75 seconds, turn the donuts over, and fry for around 75 seconds once again, until the other side looks slightly golden-brown too. With the help of a slotted spoon, take each donut out of the fryer and drain well using paper towels. Repeat the process for the rest of the donuts.
9. Roll each doughnut on all sides in the topping while they are still somewhat warm. Allow the donuts to cool on clean racks.
10. Fill a pastry bag with the filling. Insert the tip into the side of a doughnut. Squeeze the pastry bag and fill the doughnut with custard only until the center of the doughnut slightly bulges. (You are aiming to pipe a good

2 to 3 teaspoons of filling inside.) Repeat the process for the rest of the donuts and filling.

Coffee Coat Donuts

A great early morning boost!

Yield: 6 Donuts

Total Time to Prepare: 25 Minutes

Ingredients for the crumb topping:
- ¼ cup of brown sugar, light and packed
- ¼ cup of butter, unsalted and melted
- ½ tsp. of cinnamon, ground
- 1 cup of flour, all-purpose

Ingredients for the doughnuts:
- ¼ cup of sugar, granulated
- ½ cup of milk, whole
- ½ tsp. of salt
- 1 cup of flour, all-purpose
- 1 egg, large
- 1 tbsp. of butter, unsalted
- 1 tsp. of baker's style baking powder
- 1 tsp. of pure vanilla

Ingredients for the glaze:
- ½ cup of confectioner's sugar
- ½ tbsp. of milk, whole

Directions:
1. Preheat the oven to 325 degrees. As the oven heats up grease a big donut pan using cooking spray.
2. To make the crumb topping, use a moderate sized container and put in the melted butter, light brown sugar, all-purpose flour and cinnamon. Stir thoroughly until a coarse consistency is achieved. Save mixture for later.

3. Next use a moderate sized container and put in the all-purpose flour, baker's style baking powder and dash of salt. Stir thoroughly until well blended and save for later.
4. Use a big container of a stand mixer and put in the granulated sugar, large egg and melted butter. Put in the whole milk and pure vanilla. Beat on the lowermost setting until blended. Pour this mixture into the flour mixture.
5. Grease the donut cups and fill them ¾ of the way full with the donut batter. Top off with the crumb topping.
6. Put inside the oven to bake for 15 to 16 minutes or until the donuts are light gold. Take out of the oven and let it rest for 5 minutes. Move the donuts onto a wire rack to cool a little.
7. As the donuts cool, make the glaze. To do this put the confectioner's sugar and whole milk into a little container. Whisk until a smooth consistency is achieved.
8. Lightly sprinkle the glaze over the donuts and serve.

Colourful Donuts

A beautiful donut with multicoloured sprinkles!
Yield: about sixteen 3-inch doughnuts
Ingredients:

- 1 recipe Traditional Buttermilk Donuts, prepared with 3 tablespoons rainbow sprinkles folded into the batter, cut into 3-inch rings, fried, and beginning to cool
- 2 recipes Crunchy Sugar Glaze, made instantly before using
- Rainbow sprinkles

Directions:

1. Coat two rimmed baking sheet pans using aluminium foil or parchment paper.
2. Immerse the top of each doughnut into the glaze and generously scatter sprinkles on top of the glaze before it sets. Allow the donuts to sit on the readied pans until the glaze sets, about 5 minutes.

Creamy Donuts

A creamy Delight!
Yield: about twenty-six 2½-inch filled doughnuts
Ingredients:
- 1 recipe Crispy Cream Donuts or Fundamental Yeast-Raised Donuts, prepared upto the the first rise step
- 1 recipe Pastry Cream
- 2 recipes Dark Chocolate Glaze
- Pastry bag and coupler fitted with a Bismarck #230 tip

Directions:
1. Thoroughly flour two rimmed baking sheet pans. Softly punch down the dough and split it in half. Roll one piece of dough on a slightly floured work surface to ½-inch thickness. Cut out doughnuts with a slightly floured 2½-inch round cutter. Repeat the process with the rest of the dough. Slowly gather all the left-over dough, press it together, roll the dough again to the same thickness, and cut out as many additional donuts as you possibly can.
2. Place the doughnuts, well spaced, on the prepared pans. Allow to rise in a warm, draft-free location until twice its initial size, approximately half an hour.
3. Coat two rimmed baking sheet pans with a layer of three paper towels. Heat up 3 inches of oil using a deep pot or deep-fat fryer to 350° to 355°F. Once the oil has reached the desired temperature, fry a few doughnuts

at a time; do not crowd. Fry until your donuts become slightly golden brown, approximately 1½ minutes, turn the donuts over, and fry for approximately 1½ minutes more, until the other side looks slightly golden-brown too. With the help of a slotted spoon, take each donut out of the fryer and drain well using paper towels. Repeat the process for the rest of the donuts. Cool thoroughly.
4. Scrape the pastry cream into the pastry bag. Insert the tip into the side of a doughnut. Squeeze the pastry bag and fill the doughnut with pastry cream only until the center of the doughnut slightly bulges. (You are aiming to pipe a generous 2 to 3 teaspoons of filling inside.) Repeat the process for the rest of the donuts and pastry cream.
5. Immerse the top of each doughnut in the glaze and allow to sit for approximately 5 minutes to let the glaze set.

Doughnut Shop Glazed Donuts

Just like the classic donut you find in shops.
Yield: twenty-two 3-inch ring-shaped doughnuts
Ingredients:

- 1 recipe [Crispy Cream Donuts](), cut into 3-inch rings, fried, and beginning to cool

Glaze:

- 9 tablespoons unsalted butter
- 3 cups sifted confectioners' sugar
- 6 to 9 tablespoons hot water
- 2¼ teaspoons pure vanilla extract

Directions:

1. For the glaze: Melt the butter in a moderate-sized saucepan. Off the heat, whisk in the confectioners' sugar, a bit at a time, making sure it incorporates smoothly, with no lumps. Mix in the water slowly, adding only enough to reach the desired consistency. It should be slightly thick and opaque, but still fluid. Mix in the vanilla.
2. Immerse the top of each doughnut in the glaze and allow to sit for approximately 5 minutes to let the glaze set.

Espresso Overload Donuts

Yield: about twelve 3-inch doughnuts

Ingredients:

- 1 recipe Soft and Sheer Sugar Glaze, prepared whisking I tablespoon instant espresso powder with the water
- 1 recipe Sour Cream Donuts, prepared substituting 2 tablespoons instant espresso powder for the nutmeg, cut into 3-inch rings, fried, and starting to cool

Directions:

1. Immerse the top of each doughnut into the glaze and allow to sit for approximately 5 minutes to let the glaze set.

French Crullers with Grand Marnier Glaze

Yield: about nine 3-inch crullers

Ingredients:

- 1 recipe French Crullers, fried and beginning to cool

Grand Marnier glaze:

- ½ teaspoon orange flower water (optional)
- 1 cup sifted confectioners' sugar
- 1 teaspoon Grand Marnier
- 2 tablespoons milk

Directions:
1. Mix together the glaze ingredients in a small container until smooth.
2. Instantly apply the glaze all over the tops of the crullers with a pastry brush or, alternatively, immerse the tops of the crullers into the glaze. Allow to sit for 5 minutes to let the glaze set.

German Choco-Cake Donuts

A basic chocolate donut with a dense topping of coconut and pecans.

Yield: about fourteen 3-inch doughnuts

Ingredients:
- 1 recipe <u>Choco-Cake Donuts</u>, cut into 3-inch rings, baked, and beginning to cool

Topping:
- 1 teaspoon pure vanilla extract
- 1½ cups sweetened long-shred coconut
- 3 large egg yolks
- 7½ tablespoons unsalted butter, at room temperature, cut into pieces
- Scant 1 cup evaporated milk
- Scant 1 cup pecan halves, toasted and chopped
- Scant 1 cup sugar

Directions:
1. For the topping: Place the evaporated milk and sugar in a large saucepan and whisk to combine. Mix in the egg yolks and butter. Softly cook over moderate heat until the mixture reaches a simmer; continue to cook,

whisking frequently, until it thickens and slightly darkens, about 5 minutes. Turn off the heat and mix in the coconut and pecans. Cool to room temperature, stirring intermittently to release the heat. The topping may be stored for up to 3 days in an airtight container in the refrigerator. Bring to room temperature before using.
2. While the doughnuts are still somewhat warm, use a small offset spatula to spread the topping all over the tops.

Gingerbread Donuts with Lemon Glaze

These donuts have the awesome flavour of gingerbread!
Yield: about twelve 3-inch doughnuts
Ingredients:

- ¼ cup flavorless vegetable oil, such as canola, plus more for deep-frying
- ¼ teaspoon white pepper
- ½ teaspoon baking soda
- ½ teaspoon ground allspice
- ½ teaspoon salt
- ⅔ cup firmly packed dark brown sugar
- ⅔ cup full-fat sour cream, at room temperature
- 1 recipe Citrus Glaze, made with freshly squeezed lemon juice
- 1 tablespoon baking powder
- 1 tablespoon ground ginger
- 1 tablespoon plus 1 teaspoon ground cinnamon
- 1¼ cups sifted cake flour
- 1¾ cups all-purpose flour
- 2 large egg yolks, at room temperature

- 2 large eggs, at room temperature
- 6 tablespoons unsulfured molasses

Directions:
1. Mix together both flours, the cinnamon, ginger, baking powder, baking soda, salt, allspice, and white pepper in a moderate-sized container .
2. In a big container, blend the whole eggs, egg yolks, and brown sugar using an electric mixer until pale and creamy, or mix thoroughly using your hands. Put in and mix in the sour cream, molasses, and oil until well blended. Put in the dry mixture in two batches and mix using a wooden spoon only until the dough comes together. Cover and place in the fridge for minimum 2 hours or up to overnight.
3. Take the dough out of the fridge. Cover a rimmed baking sheet pan with a layer of three paper towels. Heat up 3 inches of oil using a deep pot or deep-fat fryer to 350° to 355°F.
4. As the oil heats, dust the work surface generously with flour. Scrape the dough (it will be soft) onto the surface, coat the top of the dough slightly with flour, and roll the dough until it is ½ inch thick. Cut out donuts using a slightly floured 3-inch round cutter. Slowly gather all the left-over dough, press it together, roll the dough again to the same thickness, and cut out as many additional donuts as you possibly can.
5. Fry multiple donuts simultaneously, without crowding. Fry until your donuts become slightly golden brown, approximately 1½ minutes, turn the donuts over, and fry for approximately 1½ minutes more, until the other side looks slightly golden-brown too. With the help of a slotted spoon, take each donut out of the fryer and drain well using paper towels. Repeat the process with the rest of the dough.

6. While the doughnuts are still somewhat warm, immerse the tops into the glaze or spread it using a small offset spatula. Allow to sit approximately 5 minutes to let the glaze set.

Grape Overload Donuts

The perfect donut if you love the taste of grapes!
Yield: about twenty-eight 2½-inch filled doughnuts
Ingredients:

- 1 recipe Crispy Cream Donuts or Fundamental Yeast-Raised Donuts, cut into 2½-inch rounds, fried, and beginning to cool
- 1¼ cups grape jelly or jam
- 2 recipes Soft and Sheer Sugar Glaze, using Welch's grape juice instead of water
- Pastry bag and coupler fitted with a Bismarck #230 tip
- Powdered grape beverage powder, such as Kool-Aid

Directions:
1. Scrape the jelly into the pastry bag. Insert the tip into the side of a doughnut. Squeeze the pastry bag and fill the doughnut with jelly only until the center of the doughnut slightly bulges. (You are aiming to pipe a generous 2 to 3 teaspoons of filling inside.) Repeat the process for the rest of the donuts and jelly.
2. Immerse the top of each doughnut into the glaze or spread it using a small offset spatula; you want a very sheer layer, just enough to help the powdered beverage stick. Liberally drizzle the powdered juice drink on top while the glaze is still wet. Allow to sit for approximately 5 minutes to let the glaze set.

Honey Milk Donuts

Light fluffy donuts for anyone who loves the taste of honey!
Yield: about twenty-six 2½-inch filled doughnuts

Ingredients:

- 1 recipe [Crispy Cream Donuts](#) or [Fundamental Yeast-Raised Donuts](#), prepared through the first rise

Honey pastry cream:

- ¼ cup (½ stick) unsalted butter, at room temperature, cut into pieces
- ¼ cup cornstarch
- ¼ cup honey
- ½ teaspoon pure vanilla extract
- 2 cups whole milk
- 2 large egg yolks
- 2 large eggs
- Pinch of salt

Milk and honey glaze:

- ¾ cup whole milk
- 4½ cups sifted confectioners' sugar
- 6 tablespoons honey
- Pastry bag and coupler fitted with a Bismarck #230 tip

Directions:

1. For the pastry cream: Bring the milk to a boil in a moderate-sized nonreactive saucepan over moderate heat; turn off the heat and cover to keep warm.
2. In the meantime, whisk together the whole eggs, egg yolks, and honey in a moderate-sized container until creamy. Mix in the cornstarch and salt until smooth. Pour about one-quarter of the warm milk into the egg mixture, whisking gently. Put in the remaining milk and whisk to combine. Instantly pour the mixture back into the saucepan and cook over medium-low heat. Whisk almost continuously and watch for bubbles. As soon as

the mixture begins to boil, whisk rapidly and continuously over the heat for 1 to 2 minutes. The pastry cream should be thick enough to mound when dropped from a spoon, but still be satiny. Turn off the heat and whisk in the butter and vanilla.

3. Let the pastry cream cool; mix intermittently to release the heat. When the pastry cream is almost at room temperature, scrape it into an airtight container, press plastic wrap directly onto the surface (to keep a skin from forming), snap on the lid, and refrigerate until thoroughly chilled, at least 4 hours and up to 2 days.

4. For the doughnuts: Thoroughly flour two rimmed baking sheet pans. Softly punch down the dough and split it in half. Roll one piece of dough on a slightly floured work surface to ½-inch thickness. Cut out doughnuts with a slightly floured 2½-inch round cutter. Repeat the process with the rest of the dough. Slowly gather all the left-over dough, press it together, roll the dough again to the same thickness, and cut out as many additional donuts as you possibly can. Place the doughnuts, well spaced, on the prepared pans. Allow to rise in a warm, draft-free location until twice its initial size, approximately half an hour.

5. Coat two rimmed baking sheet pans with a layer of three paper towels. Heat up 3 inches of oil using a deep pot or deep-fat fryer to 350° to 355°F. Once the oil has reached the desired temperature, fry a few doughnuts at a time; do not crowd. Fry until your donuts become slightly golden brown, approximately 1½ minutes, turn the donuts over, and fry for approximately 1½ minutes more, until the other side looks slightly golden-brown too. With the help of a slotted spoon, take each donut out of the fryer and drain well using paper towels.

Repeat the process for the rest of the donuts. Cool thoroughly.
6. Scrape the pastry cream into the pastry bag. Insert the tip into the side of a cooled doughnut. Squeeze the pastry bag and fill the doughnut with pastry cream only until the center of the doughnut slightly bulges. (You are aiming to pipe a generous 2 to 3 teaspoons of filling inside.) Repeat the process for the rest of the donuts and pastry cream.
7. For the glaze: Place the milk and honey in a small saucepan and heat over low heat only until warm, stirring to dissolve the honey. Remove from the heat. Place the confectioners' sugar in a moderate-sized container and whisk in the warm honey mixture until smooth.
8. Immerse the top of each doughnut in the glaze and allow to sit for approximately 5 minutes to let the glaze set.

Jammed Donuts

Love jam? These donuts are for you!

Yield: 18 to 20 Donuts

Total Time to Prepare: 2 Hours and 40 Minutes

Ingredients:
- ½ tsp. of salt
- 1 cup of milk, lukewarm
- 2 ½ tsp. of yeast, active and dry
- 2 eggs, large and beaten
- 2 tbsp. of butter, unsalted, melted and cooled slightly
- 2 tbsp. of sugar
- 4 to 4 ½ cups of flour, all-purpose
- Powdered sugar, for dusting

- Strawberry jam
- Vegetable oil, for frying

Directions:
1. Use a big container and put in the all-purpose flour and dash of salt. Stir to mix and put in the yeast. Stir again.
2. Put in the whole milk and sugar. Allow to sit for 5 to 10 minutes or until foamy. Stir thoroughly to incorporate.
3. Put in the large eggs and cooled butter. Stir again to uniformly incorporate.
4. Place the dough onto a slightly floured surface. Knead for 1 to 2 minutes or until the dough is smooth. Move into a big container that has been greased. Cover and save for later to rise for 2 hours or until the donut dough has doubled in size.
5. Punch down the dough after this time and knead for 1 minute.
6. Roll out the donut dough until ½ inch in thickness. Cut out 3 to 4 inch thick rounds from the dough and put over two big baking sheets. Allow to rest and rise for 20 minutes or until it becomes twice as big.
7. Fill a deep fat fryer with three inches of vegetable oil. Heat the oil until it achieves a temperature of 350 degrees. Once the oil is hot enough put in the donuts. Fry for 5 minutes or until the donuts seem golden. Take out and put over large plate coated with paper towels to drain.
8. After draining, fill a large pastry bag with the strawberry jam. Fit the tip of the pastry bag into the donut. Fill the donut with the jam until plump. Repeat with the rest of the.
9. Dust with powdered sugar before serving.

Jamy Donuts

Who doesn't like jelly and jam on their donuts?
Yield: about twenty-six 2½-inch filled doughnuts
Ingredients:
- 1 recipe Crispy Cream Donuts or Fundamental Yeast-Raised Donuts, prepared through the first rise
- 1¼ cups jam, fruit preserve, or jelly of your choice
- Pastry bag and coupler fitted with a Bismarck #230 tip
- Superfine, granulated, or confectioners' sugar

Directions:
1. Thoroughly flour two rimmed baking sheet pans. Softly punch down the dough and split it in half.
2. If using a chunky jam or fruit preserve: Roll one piece of dough on a slightly floured work surface to ½-inch thickness. Cut out dough rounds with a slightly floured 2½-inch round cutter. Repeat the process with the rest of the dough. Slowly gather all the left-over dough, press it together, roll out the dough, and cut out as many additional rounds as possible. Make sure you end up with an even number. Using two cereal spoons, dollop about 2 teaspoons of jam in the centers of half of the dough rounds. Immerse a pastry brush in room-temperature water and lightly brush the edges of the dough around the jam. Place a plain round on top of each filled round and press the edges together with your fingertips to seal them well.
3. If using a smooth jelly: Roll one piece of dough on a slightly floured work surface to ½-inch thickness. Cut out doughnuts with a slightly floured 2½-inch round cutter. Repeat the process with the rest of the dough. Slowly gather all the left-over dough, press it together, roll the dough again to the same thickness, and cut out as many additional donuts as you possibly can.

4. Place the doughnuts, well spaced, on the prepared pans. Allow to rise in a warm, draft-free location until twice its initial size, approximately half an hour
5. Coat two rimmed baking sheet pans with a layer of three paper towels. Heat up 3 inches of oil using a deep pot or deep-fat fryer to 350° to 355°F. Once the oil has reached the desired temperature, fry a few doughnuts at a time; do not crowd. Fry until your donuts become slightly golden brown, approximately 1½ minutes, turn the donuts over, and fry for approximately 1½ minutes more, until the other side looks slightly golden-brown too. With the help of a slotted spoon, take each donut out of the fryer and drain well using paper towels. Repeat the process for the rest of the donuts.
6. For chunky jam-filled doughnuts: While the doughnuts are still warm, toss them in the sugar of your choice to cover completely.
7. For smooth jelly-filled doughnuts: While the doughnuts are still warm, roll them on all sides in the sugar of your choice to cover completely. Allow the donuts to cool. Scrape the jelly into the pastry bag. Insert the tip into the side of a doughnut. Squeeze the pastry bag and fill the doughnut with jelly only until the center of the doughnut slightly bulges. (You are aiming to pipe a generous 2 to 3 teaspoons of filling inside.) Repeat the process for the rest of the donuts.

Kid's Party Donuts

These colourful and sweet donuts are a hit at any kids' party!
Yield: **8 Donuts**
Total Time to Prepare: **30 Minutes**
Ingredients for the donuts:

- ¼ cup of milk, whole

- ¼ cup of sugar, granulated
- ¼ cup of yogurt, Greek
- ¼ tsp. of baker's style baking soda
- ¼ tsp. of nutmeg, ground
- ¼ tsp. of salt
- ½ cup of rainbow sprinkles
- 1 ½ tsp. of pure vanilla
- 1 cup of flour, all-purpose
- 1 egg, large
- 1 tbsp. of brown sugar, light and packed
- 1 tsp. of baker's style baking powder
- 2 tbsp. of butter, unsalted and melted

Ingredients for the glaze:

- ¼ cup of milk, whole
- 1 tsp. of pure vanilla
- 2 cups of confectioner's sugar
- Rainbow sprinkles, for topping and optional

Directions:

1. Preheat the oven to 350 degrees. As the oven heats up grease a big donut pan using cooking spray.
2. Use a moderate sized container and put in the all-purpose flour, baker's style baking powder and soda, dash of salt, nutmeg, sugar and light brown sugar. Stir thoroughly until well blended and set this mixture aside.
3. Use a big container and put in the whole milk, Greek yogurt and large egg. Stir thoroughly for 1 minute or until a smooth consistency is achieved. Put in the melted butter and pure vanilla. Whisk until blended.
4. Add the milk mixture into the flour mixture. Stir thoroughly until just blended. Put in the sprinkles and fold gently to incorporate.
5. Fill each donut cup in the pan ¾ of the way full with the batter.

6. Put inside the oven to bake for 10 mins or until golden. Remove and save for later to cool.
7. As the donuts cool, make the glaze. To do this place a medium saucepan over low heat. Put in the pure vanilla, whole milk and confectioner's sugar. Whisk until a smooth consistency is achieved. Remove from heat.
8. Immerse every baked donut in the glaze and sprinkle the rainbow sprinkles over each donut. Allow some time for the glaze to set and serve.

Lemon Blast Donuts

This donut is for all the lemon lovers out there!
Yield: about thirteen 2½-inch doughnuts
Ingredients:
- ½ a recipe Crispy Cream Donuts or Fundamental Yeast-Raised Donuts, prepared through the first rise
- Pastry bag and coupler fitted with a Bismarck #230 tip
- Pastry bag and coupler fitted with a large star tip, such as Ateco #847

Lemon curd:
- ¼ cup freshly squeezed lemon juice
- ½ teaspoon finely grated lemon zest (optional)
- ¾ cup sugar
- 1 large egg yolk
- 2 large eggs
- 6 tablespoons (¾ stick) unsalted butter, at room temperature, cut into pieces

Meringue:
- 1 cup sugar
- 4 large egg whites
- Heaping ¼ teaspoon cream of tartar

Directions:

1. For the lemon curd: Place the lemon juice, whole eggs, egg yolk, and sugar in the top of a double boiler. Whisk to break up the eggs. Put in the butter. Fill the bottom of the double boiler with enough hot water to just reach the bottom of the top pan; place the top pan over the bottom pan. Place the double boiler over moderate heat and bring the water to a simmer.
2. Whisk the mixture often over the simmering water until it reaches 180°F on a thermometer. (The temperature is more important than the time it takes; the mixture should not simmer.) The curd will thicken and form a soft shape when dropped by a spoon. If desired, mix in the lemon zest after removing from the heat. Cool the curd to room temperature, scrape it into an airtight container, place a piece of plastic wrap directly onto the surface (to keep a skin from forming), and refrigerate until chilled, at least 4 hours or up to 1 week.
3. Thoroughly flour a rimmed baking sheet pan. Softly punch down the dough and split it in half. Roll one piece of dough on a slightly floured work surface to ½-inch thickness. Cut out doughnuts with a slightly floured 2½-inch round cutter. Repeat the process with the rest of the dough. Slowly gather all the left-over dough, press it together, roll the dough again to the same thickness, and cut out as many additional donuts as you possibly can. Place the doughnuts, well spaced, on the prepared pan. Allow to rise in a warm, draft-free location until twice its initial size, approximately half an hour.
4. Cover a rimmed baking sheet pan with a layer of three paper towels. Heat up 3 inches of oil using a deep pot or deep-fat fryer to 350° to 355°F. Once the oil has reached the desired temperature, fry a few doughnuts at a time; do not crowd. Fry until your donuts become slightly golden brown, approximately 1½ minutes, turn

the donuts over, and fry for approximately 1½ minutes more, until the other side looks slightly golden-brown too. With the help of a slotted spoon, take each donut out of the fryer and drain well using paper towels. Repeat the process for the rest of the donuts. Cool thoroughly.

5. Scrape the lemon curd into a pastry bag fitted with a coupler and a #230 tip. Insert the tip into the top of doughnut. Squeeze the pastry bag and fill the doughnut with lemon curd only until the center of the doughnut slightly bulges. (You are aiming to pipe a generous 2 to 3 teaspoons of filling inside.) Repeat the process for the rest of the donuts and lemon curd.

6. For the meringue: Mix together the egg whites and sugar in the top of a double boiler. Fill the bottom of the double boiler with enough hot water to just reach the bottom of the top pan; place the top pan over the bottom pan. Place the double boiler over moderate heat and bring the water to a boil, whisking the egg whites intermittently. As the temperature nears 140°F, whisk frequently. When the temperature reaches 160°F, turn off the heat, put in the cream of tartar, and beat on high speed with a handheld electric mixer right in the pot until a thick meringue forms. (Alternatively, you can transfer the mixture to a stand mixer and beat with the balloon whip attachment). Keep beating the meringue until it cools to a barely warm temperature, about 5 minutes.

7. Instantly scrape the meringue into a clean pastry bag fitted with a large star tip. Pipe a generous swirl of meringue on top of each doughnut, covering the hole where you inserted the lemon curd. Brown the meringue with a mini propane torch.

Lemon Overload Donuts

Yield: sixteen to eighteen 3-inch doughnuts, depending on recipe chosen

Ingredients:
- 1 recipe Traditional Buttermilk Donuts or Mashed Potato Donuts, prepared with 1 tablespoon finely minced lemon zest added to the batter, cut into 3-inch rings, fried, and beginning to cool
- 1 tablespoon finely minced lemon zest
- 2 recipes Citrus Glaze, made with freshly squeezed lemon juice

Directions:
1. Coat two rimmed baking sheet pans using aluminium foil or parchment paper.
2. Whisk the lemon zest into the freshly prepared glaze. Immerse the top of each doughnut into the glaze or spread it using a small offset spatula. Allow the donuts to sit on the readied pans until the glaze sets, about 5 minutes

Macon Donuts

Maple Bacon donuts? Does this combination even work? Only one way to find out!

Yield: 6 Donuts
Total Time to Prepare: 25 Minutes
Ingredients:
- ¼ cup of brown sugar, light and packed
- ¼ cup of sour cream
- ¼ tsp. of salt
- 1 cup of flour, all-purpose
- 1 egg, large and beaten
- 1 tsp. of baker's style baking powder

- 1 tsp. of pure vanilla
- 2 tbsp. of butter, unsalted and soft
- 2 tbsp. of milk, whole

Ingredients for the glaze:

- 1 cup of sugar, powdered
- 3 strips of bacon, brown sugar and maple and chopped
- 3 to 4 tbsp. of maple syrup

Directions:

1. Preheat the oven to 325 degrees.
2. Use a big container and put in the all-purpose flour, baker's style baking powder and dash of salt. Stir thoroughly and set this mixture aside.
3. Use a different big container and put in the butter and sugar. Beat with an electric mixer on the highest setting until creamy in consistency. Put in the large egg, sour cream, pure vanilla and whole milk. Continue to beat until uniformly mixed.
4. Pour the butter mixture into the flour mixture. Stir thoroughly until blended.
5. Pour the batter into the donut pan, making sure to fill each donut cup ¾ of the way full.
6. Put inside the oven to bake for 12 to 15 minutes or until the donuts are thoroughly baked. Take out of the oven and move to a wire rack to cool completely.
7. As the donuts cool, make the glaze. To do this use a little container and put in the powdered sugar and maple syrup. Whisk until a smooth consistency is achieved.
8. Once the donuts are cooled, dip each donut into the glaze. Top off with the bacon and save for later to set. Serve.

Macon Donuts

Maple syrup and bacon go great on donuts together!
Yield: about thirty 4-inch log-shaped doughnuts
Ingredients:

- 1 recipe [Crispy Cream Donuts](#) or [Fundamental Yeast-Raised Donuts](#), prepared through the first rise
- 24 slices bacon, cooked until crisp and cut or broken into ½-inch pieces

Maple glaze:

- ¾ cup pure maple syrup
- 3 cups sifted confectioners' sugar

Directions:

1. Thoroughly flour two rimmed baking sheet pans. Softly punch down the dough and split it in half. Roll one piece of dough on a slightly floured work surface into a rectangle ½ inch thick. Use a pizza wheel to cut the dough into 4 × 1½-inch strips. Repeat the process with the rest of the dough. Place the strips, well spaced, on the prepared pans. Allow to rise in a warm, draft-free location until twice its initial size, approximately half an hour.
2. Coat two rimmed baking sheet pans with a layer of three paper towels. Heat up 3 inches of oil using a deep pot or deep-fat fryer to 350° to 355°F. Once the oil has reached the desired temperature, fry a few logs at a time; do not crowd. Fry until your donuts become slightly golden brown, approximately 1 minute and 20 seconds, turn the donuts over, and fry for approximately 1 minute and 20 seconds more, until the other side looks slightly golden-brown too. With the help of a slotted spoon, remove each log from the oil and drain well using paper towels. Repeat with the remaining logs. Cool until just barely warm to the touch.

3. 3. For the glaze: Heat the maple syrup in a moderate sized saucepan set over medium-low heat only until it is warm, 2 to 3 minutes. Turn off the heat and whisk in the confectioners' sugar until totally smooth. Immerse the top of each log in the glaze or spread it with a small offset spatula. Scatter crisp bacon pieces on top and allow to sit for approximately 5 minutes to let the glaze set.

Maple Donuts

These donuts go great in the morning with a freshly brewed cup of coffee.

Yield: 8 Donuts

Total Time to Prepare: 25 Minutes

Ingredients for the maple donuts:

- ¼ cup of maple syrup
- ½ cup of butter, soft
- ¾ cup of buttermilk
- 1 tbsp. of cinnamon
- 1 tsp. of nutmeg
- 1 tsp. of pure vanilla
- 2 cups of flour, all-purpose
- 2 eggs, large
- 2 tsp. of baker's style baking powder

Ingredients for the maple glaze:

- ½ cup of maple syrup
- 1 cup of confectioner's sugar
- 1 tbsp. of butter, melted
- 2 tsp. of cinnamon

Directions:

1. Preheat the oven to 350 degrees. As the oven heats up grease a big donut pan using cooking spray.

2. Use a big container and put in the all-purpose flour, cinnamon, ground nutmeg and baker's style baking powder. Stir to mix.
3. Use a different big container and put in the buttermilk, large egg, soft butter, pure vanilla and maple syrup. Whisk until uniformly mixed.
4. Pour the maple syrup mixture into the flour mixture. Stir thoroughly until just blended.
5. Pour the batter into the greased donut pan, making sure to fill each donut cup ¾ of the way full.
6. Put inside the oven to bake for 15 minutes or until the donuts are thoroughly baked. Take out of the oven and move to a wire rack to cool completely.
7. As the donuts cool make the maple glaze. To do this add all of the ingredients for the glaze into a medium bowl. Whisk until a smooth consistency is achieved.
8. Immerse one side of each donut into the glaze. Place back onto the wire rack for the glaze to set. Serve.

Marshnut Donuts

Marshmallow cream and peanut butter taste great together!
Yield: about twenty-six 2½-inch filled doughnuts
Ingredients:
- 1 cup plus 2 tablespoons marshmallow creme, such as Fluff
- 1 recipe Crispy Cream Donuts or Fundamental Yeast-Raised Donuts, prepared through the first rise
- 1 recipe Peanut Butter Glaze

Directions:
1. Thoroughly flour two rimmed baking sheet pans. Softly punch down the dough and split it in half. Roll one piece of dough on a slightly floured work surface to ½-inch thickness. Cut out dough rounds with a slightly floured

2½-inch round cutter. Repeat the process with the rest of the dough. Slowly gather all the left-over dough, press it together, roll out the dough, and cut out as many additional rounds as possible. Make sure you end up with an even number.

2. Using two cereal spoons, dollop about 2 teaspoons of marshmallow creme in the centers of half of the dough rounds. Immerse a pastry brush in room-tempera ture water and lightly brush the edges of the dough around the marshmallow filling. Place a plain round on top of each filled round and press the edges together with your fingertips to seal them well.
3. Place the doughnuts, well spaced, on the prepared pans. Allow to rise in a warm, draft-free location until twice its initial size, approximately half an hour.
4. Coat two rimmed baking sheet pans with a layer of three paper towels. Heat up 3 inches of oil using a deep pot or deep-fat fryer to 350° to 355°F. Once the oil has reached the desired temperature, fry a few doughnuts at a time; do not crowd. Fry until your donuts become slightly golden brown, approximately 1½ minutes, turn the donuts over, and fry for approximately 1½ minutes more, until the other side looks slightly golden-brown too. With the help of a slotted spoon, take each donut out of the fryer and drain well using paper towels. Repeat the process for the rest of the donuts.
5. While the doughnuts are still somewhat warm, immerse the tops into the glaze or spread it using a small offset spatula. Allow to sit for approximately 5 minutes to let the glaze set.

Nuteja Donuts

These donuts are filled with Nutella, and have the delicious gianduja ganache on top!

Yield: about twenty-six 2½-inch doughnuts

Ingredients:
- ¾ cup plus 2 tablespoons heavy cream
- 1 recipe Crispy Cream Donuts or Fundamental Yeast-Raised Donuts, prepared through the first rise
- 1¼ cups Nutella
- 14 ounces milk chocolate gianduja, such as Callebaut, finely chopped
- Gianduja ganache:

Directions:
1. Thoroughly flour two rimmed baking sheet pans. Softly punch down the dough and split it in half. Roll one piece of dough on a slightly floured work surface to ½-inch thickness. Cut out dough rounds with a slightly floured 2½-inch round cutter. Repeat the process with the rest of the dough. Slowly gather all the left-over dough, press it together, roll out the dough, and cut out as many additional rounds as possible. Make sure you end up with an even number.
2. Using two cereal spoons, dollop about 2 teaspoons of Nutella in the centers of half of the dough rounds. Immerse a pastry brush in room-temperature water and lightly brush the edges of the dough around the Nutella filling. Place a plain round on top of each filled round and press the edges together with your fin gertips to seal them well.
3. Place the doughnuts, well spaced, on the prepared pans. Allow to rise in a warm, draft-free location until twice its initial size, approximately half an hour.

4. While the doughnuts are rising, make the ganache: Bring the cream to a boil in a large saucepan over moderate heat. Turn off the heat and instantly sprinkle the gianduja into the cream. Cover and allow to sit for 5 minutes. Softly mix the ganache until smooth—the heat of the cream should melt the gianduja. If the gianduja does not melt completely, place the pan over very low heat and mix the ganache frequently, until melted, taking care not to burn it. Cool until warm but still fluid.
5. While the ganache is cooling, line 2 rimmed baking sheet pans with a layer of three paper towels. Heat up 3 inches of oil using a deep pot or deep-fat fryer to 350° to 355°F. Once the oil has reached the desired temperature, fry a few doughnuts at a time; do not crowd. Fry until your donuts become slightly golden brown, approximately 1½ minutes, turn the donuts over, and fry for approximately 1½ minutes more, until the other side looks slightly golden-brown too. With the help of a slotted spoon, take each donut out of the fryer and drain well using paper towels. Repeat the process for the rest of the donuts.
6. While the doughnuts are still somewhat warm, immerse the tops in the ganache. Allow to sit for approximately 5 minutes to allow the ganache to set.

Oreo Cream Donuts

Love the taste of Oreo cookies? These donuts might just be for you!
Yield: 6 Donuts
Total Time to Prepare: 20 Minutes
Ingredients for the donuts:
- ¼ cup of cocoa, powdered
- ½ cup of brown sugar, light and packed

- ½ cup of milk, whole
- ½ tsp. of pure vanilla
- ½ tsp. of salt
- 1 cup of flour, all-purpose
- 1 egg, large
- 1 tsp. of baker's style baking powder
- 2 ½ tbsp. of butter, unsalted and melted

Ingredients for the cream cheese frosting:
- ¼ tsp. of pure vanilla
- 1 ½ cups of confectioner's sugar
- 1 cup of Oreo cookies, chopped and for topping
- 1 to 2 tbsp. of milk, whole
- 2 tbsp. of butter, unsalted and soft
- 4 ounces of cream cheese, soft

Directions:
1. Preheat the oven to 350 degrees. As the oven heats up grease a big donut pan.
2. Use a big container and put in the all-purpose flour, light brown sugar, dash of salt, powdered cocoa and baker's style baking powder. Stir thoroughly until well blended.
3. Put in the pure vanilla, large egg, melted butter and whole milk. Lightly stir until uniformly mixed.
4. Pour the batter in the donut pan, making sure to fill each donut cup ¾ of the way full.
5. Put inside the oven to bake for 10 mins or until the donuts are thoroughly baked. Take out of the oven and move to a wire rack to cool completely.
6. While the donuts are cooking make the frosting. To do this use a big container and put in all of the ingredients for the frosting except for the Oreo cookies. Beat with an electric mixer until a smooth consistency is achieved.
7. Spread the frosting onto each of the donuts, making sure to spread it uniformly.

8. Top off with the Oreo cookies and serve.

Peachcan Fritters

Peaches and Pecans go great great together!
Yield: about 30 golf ball-size fritters

Ingredients:
- ½ cup pecan halves, chopped
- 1 recipe batter for Sour Cream Donuts
- 1½ cups diced (½-inch) peeled peaches (from about 4 medium peaches)
- Flavorless vegetable oil for deep-frying, such as canola

Brown sugar glaze:
- ½ teaspoon freshly squeezed lemon juice
- ¾ cup firmly packed light brown sugar
- 4½ tablespoons unsalted butter
- 6 tablespoons heavy cream
- Pinch of salt

Directions:
1. For the glaze: Place all of the glaze ingredients in a moderate sized saucepan and whisk to combine. Bring to a boil over moderate heat, whisking intermittently, and boil until the sugar is dissolved and the mixture is smooth, 1 to 2 minutes. Turn off the heat and transfer to a container to speed up cooling. Let cool to room temperature; it will thicken slightly.
2. Cover a rimmed baking sheet pan with a layer of three paper towels. Heat up 3 inches of oil using a deep pot or deep-fat fryer to 350° to 355°F.
3. As the oil heats, fold the peaches and pecans into the doughnut batter.
4. Use a 1 9/16-inch ice cream scoop to drop the batter (carefully) into the oil. Alternatively, you can make small rounds by scooping batter with one tablespoon and

scraping it off into the oil with another tablespoon. Fry a few fritters at a time; do not crowd. Fry until you see the donuts get a golden-brown colour, approximately 1 minute and 40 seconds, turn the donuts over, and fry for approximately 1 minute and 40 seconds more, until you see the donuts get the golden-brown colour on the other side too. With the help of a slotted spoon, remove each fritter from the oil and drain well using paper towels. Repeat with the remaining batter.
5. Drizzle the glaze over the fritters or immerse each one into the glaze for a more generous amount of topping.

Peanut Jelly Donuts

The delicious combination of peanut butter and jelly!
Yield: depends on recipe chosen
Ingredients:
- 1 recipe <u>Fundamental Yeast-Raised Donuts</u>, <u>Crispy Cream Donuts</u>, or <u>Yeast-Raised Choco Donuts</u>, prepared through the first rise
- 1¼ to 2¼ cups jam, fruit preserve, or jelly of your choice (I like grape or seedless raspberry; the actual amount depends on the doughnut recipe chosen.)
- 1½ recipes <u>Peanut Butter Glaze</u>

Directions:
1. Thoroughly flour two rimmed baking sheet pans. Softly punch down the dough and split it in half.
2. Roll out the dough and either fill then fry the doughnuts (if using a chunky jam) or fry then fill the doughnuts (if using a smooth jelly) as directed in steps 2–4 of Jamy Donuts. Allow the donuts to cool.
3. Coat two rimmed baking sheet pans using aluminium foil or parchment paper. Immerse the top of each doughnut in the glaze or spread it using a small offset

spatula. (If there is extra glaze, immerse more of the doughnuts' surface, if you like.) Allow the donuts to sit on the readied pans until the glaze sets, about 5 minutes.

Pineapple-Colada Donuts
The awesome combo of pina colada and pineapple.
Yield: approximately 14 pineapple-filled doughnuts
Ingredients:

- 1 recipe [Crispy Cream Donuts](#) or [Fundamental Yeast-Raised Donuts](#), prepared through the first rise
- 2 20-ounce cans pineapple rings, packed in 100% juice (not syrup), drained, juice reserved, and rings patted dry
- Flavorless vegetable oil for deep-frying, such as canola

Pineapple rum glaze:

- 1½ cups lightly packed sweetened longshred coconut
- 3 cups sifted confectioners' sugar
- 3 tablespoons golden rum or additional pineapple juice reserved from canned pineapple
- 3 tablespoons pineapple juice, reserved from canned pineapple

Directions:

1. Thoroughly flour two rimmed baking sheet pans. Softly punch down the dough and split it in half. Roll out one piece on a slightly floured work surface to about ¼-inch thickness. Cut out dough rounds with a slightly floured 3 ⅛-inch round cutter. Repeat the process with the rest of the dough. Slowly gather all the left-over dough, press it together, roll out the dough, and cut out as many additional rounds as possible. Make sure you end up with an even number.
2. Be super cautious with this step, as it is vital. Take a dough round and pat it out so that it is about ½ inch

larger all the way around than the pineapple ring. Place a pineapple ring in the center. Immerse a pastry brush in room-temperature water and slightly brush the edges of the dough around the pineapple. Pat out another dough round to stretch it a bit, put it on top of the pineapple, align the edges of the two dough rounds, and use your fingers to press them together and seal the rounds all the way around. Flour the ⅞-inch cutter and cut out the center of the doughnut. Repeat the process with the rest of the dough rounds and pineapple rings.

3. Place the doughnuts, well spaced, on the prepared pans. Allow to rise in a warm, draft-free location until twice its initial size, approximately half an hour.

4. Coat two rimmed baking sheet pans with a layer of three paper towels. Heat up 3 inches of oil using a deep pot or deep-fat fryer to 350° to 355°F. Once the oil has reached the desired temperature, fry a few doughnuts at a time; do not crowd. Fry until your donuts become slightly golden brown, approximately 1½ minutes, turn the donuts over, and fry for approximately 1½ minutes more, until the other side looks slightly golden-brown too. With the help of a slotted spoon, take each donut out of the fryer and drain well using paper towels. Repeat the process for the rest of the donuts. Cool until just barely warm to the touch.

5. For the glaze: Mix together the pineapple juice and rum in a small container. Place the confectioners' sugar in a medium container and whisk in the liquid, a little bit at a time, until the desired consistency is reached. Immerse the top of each doughnut in the glaze and sprinkle generously with the coconut while the glaze is still wet. Allow to sit for approximately 5 minutes to let the glaze set.

Peppermint Mocha Donuts

Easy and quick to make, these donuts are great for entertaining those unannounced guests!

Yield: 6 Donuts

Total Time to Prepare: 25 Minutes

Ingredients for the donuts:
- ¼ cup + 2 tbsp. of milk, whole
- ¼ cup of Greek yogurt
- ¼ cup of sugar, granulated
- ¼ tsp. of salt
- ½ tsp. of baker's style baking soda
- ¾ cup + 1 tbsp. of flour, all-purpose
- 1 egg, large
- 1 tbsp. of brown sugar, light and packed
- 1 tbsp. of butter, unsalted, melted and cooled
- 1 tsp. of baker's style baking powder
- 1 tsp. of pure vanilla
- 1/3 cup of cocoa, powdered
- 4 tsp. of instant espresso, powdered

Ingredients for the peppermint glaze:
- ¼ tsp. of peppermint extract
- 1 ½ cups of sugar, powdered
- 2 tbsp. of milk, whole
- 2 tbsp. of peppermint candies, crushed

Directions:
1. Preheat the oven to 350 degrees. As the oven heats up grease a big donut pan using cooking spray.
2. Use a moderate sized container and put in the all-purpose flour, powdered cocoa, powdered espresso, baker's style baking powder and soda, dash of salt, granulated sugar and light brown sugar. Stir thoroughly until well blended.

3. Use a different moderate sized container and put in the Greek style yogurt, whole milk, large egg and pure vanilla. Stir thoroughly until a smooth consistency is achieved. Put in the melted butter and stir thoroughly to incorporate.
4. Add the yogurt mixture into the dry ingredients. Stir thoroughly until just blended.
5. Pour the batter in the donut pan, making sure to fill each donut cup ¾ of the way full.
6. Put inside the oven to bake for 10 mins or until the donuts are thoroughly baked. Take out of the oven and move to a wire rack to cool completely.
7. As the donuts cool, make the glaze. To do this add the powdered sugar and whole milk into a little container. Put in the peppermint extract and whisk until a smooth consistency is achieved.
8. Once the donuts are cooled dip them into the glaze and save for later for the glaze to set.
9. Top off with the crushed peppermint candies and serve.

PumpSpice Donuts

Spice and pumpkin go great together!
Yield: about sixteen 3-inch doughnuts
Ingredients:
- ½ cup firmly packed light brown sugar
- ½ cup full-fat sour cream, at room temperature
- ½ cup granulated sugar
- ½ teaspoon baking soda
- ½ teaspoon freshly grated nutmeg
- ½ teaspoon ground ginger
- 1 cup canned pumpkin puree
- 1 cup plus 2 tablespoons sifted cake flour
- 1 tablespoon plus 1 teaspoon baking powder

- 1 teaspoon ground cinnamon
- 1 teaspoon salt
- 2 large eggs, at room temperature
- 2 tablespoons flavorless vegetable oil, such as canola, plus more for deep-frying
- 3 cups all-purpose flour
- Glaze(s) or topping(s) of your choice

Directions:

1. Mix together both flours, the baking powder, cinnamon, salt, baking soda, ginger, and nutmeg in a moderate-sized container .
2. In a big container, blend the pumpkin puree, eggs, and both sugars using an electric mixer until creamy, or mix thoroughly using your hands. Put in and mix in the sour cream and 2 tablespoons oil until well blended. Put in the dry mixture in two batches and mix using a wooden spoon only until the dough comes together. Cover and place in the fridge for minimum 2 hours or up to overnight.
3. Take the dough out of the fridge. Cover a rimmed baking sheet pan with a layer of three paper towels. Heat up 3 inches of oil using a deep pot or deep-fat fryer to 350° to 355°F.
4. As the oil heats, lightly cover the work surface with flour. Place the dough on the readied surface, coat the top of the dough slightly with flour, and roll the dough until it is ½ inch thick. Cut out donuts using a slightly floured 3-inch round cutter. Slowly gather all the leftover dough, press it together, roll the dough again to the same thickness, and cut out as many additional donuts as you possibly can.
5. Fry multiple donuts simultaneously, without crowding. Fry until your donuts become slightly golden brown, approximately 1½ minutes, turn the donuts over, and

fry for approximately 1½ minutes more, until the other side looks slightly golden-brown too. With the help of a slotted spoon, take each donut out of the fryer and drain well using paper towels. Repeat the process with the rest of the dough.
6. While the doughnuts are still somewhat warm, apply dry topping(s) or glaze(s) as you wish.

Radiant Vanilla Donuts

Vanilla is one of the most popular flavours out there. This book wouldn't be complete without a good vanilla donut.

Yield: 12 Donuts
Total Time to Prepare: 20 Minutes
Ingredients:

- ¼ tsp. of nutmeg
- ½ tsp. of pure vanilla
- ¾ cup of buttermilk
- ¾ cup of sugar, granulated
- 1 cup of confectioner's sugar
- 1 tsp. of salt
- 2 cups of flour, cake
- 2 eggs, large and beaten
- 2 tbsp. of butter, melted
- 2 tbsp. of milk, whole
- 2 tsp. of baker's style baking powder

Directions:

1. Preheat the oven to 425 degrees. As the oven heats up grease a big donut pan using cooking spray.
2. Use a big container and put in the cake flour, granulated sugar, baker's style baking powder, nutmeg and dash of salt. Stir thoroughly until well blended.
3. Put in the buttermilk, large eggs and melted butter. Stir again until just blended.

4. Pour the batter into the donut pan, making sure to fill each donut cup ¾ of the way full.
5. Put inside the oven to bake for 10 mins or until the donuts are thoroughly baked. Take out of the oven and move to a wire rack to cool completely.
6. As the donuts cool, make the vanilla glaze. To do this use a little container and put in the confectioner's sugar and whole milk. Whisk until a smooth consistency is achieved.
7. Immerse the donuts into the glaze and set back onto the wire rack and let it set. Serve.

Raspberry-Fraîche Donuts

Crème fraîche and fresh raspberries make a delicious combo in a donut!

Yield: about twenty-six 2½-inch filled doughnuts

Ingredients:

- 1 pint fresh raspberries (You will need 50 to 80 raspberries, depending on their size.)
- 1 recipe Crispy Cream Donuts or Fundamental Yeast-Raised Donuts, prepared through the first rise
- 1¼ cups crème fraîche
- Flavorless vegetable oil for deep-frying, such as canola
- Superfine sugar

Directions:

1. Thoroughly flour two rimmed baking sheet pans. Softly punch down the dough and split it in half. Roll one piece of dough on a slightly floured work surface to ¼-inch thickness. Cut out dough rounds with a slightly floured 2½-inch round cutter. Repeat the process with the rest of the dough. Slowly gather all the left-over dough, press it together, roll out the dough, and cut out as

many additional rounds as possible. Make sure you end up with an even number.
2. Using two cereal spoons, dollop about 2 teaspoons of crème fraîche in the centers of half of the dough rounds. Press 2 or 3 raspberries (depending on their size) into the crème fraîche. Immerse a pastry brush in room-temperature water and lightly brush the edges of the dough around the filling. Place a plain round on top of each filled round and press the edges together with your fin gertips to seal them well.
3. Place the doughnuts, well spaced, on the prepared pans. Allow to rise in a warm, draft-free location until twice its initial size, approximately half an hour.
4. Coat two rimmed baking sheet pans with a layer of three paper towels. Heat up 3 inches of oil using a deep pot or deep-fat fryer to 350° to 355°F. Once the oil has reached the desired temperature, fry a few doughnuts at a time; do not crowd. Fry until your donuts become slightly golden brown, approximately 1½ minutes, turn the donuts over, and fry for approximately 1½ minutes more, until the other side looks slightly golden-brown too. With the help of a slotted spoon, take each donut out of the fryer and drain well using paper towels. Repeat the process for the rest of the donuts. Cool until barely warm.
5. Toss the doughnuts in superfine sugar to coat completely.

Red Velvet Donuts

The classis red colour and the delicious cocoa flavour!
Yield: about nine 3-inch doughnuts
Ingredients:
- ¼ teaspoon baking soda

- ½ a recipe Cream Cheese Frosting
- ½ teaspoon pure vanilla extract
- ¾ cup buttermilk, at room temperature
- ¾ cup sifted cake flour
- ¾ cup sugar
- 1 large egg, at room temperature
- 1 teaspoon red food coloring (gel or liquid)
- 1 teaspoon salt
- 1¾ cups plus 3 tablespoons all-purpose flour
- 2 large egg yolks, at room temperature
- 2 tablespoons sifted Dutch-processed cocoa powder
- 2 teaspoons baking powder
- 3 tablespoons unsalted butter, melted and cooled
- Flavorless vegetable oil for deep-frying, such as canola

Directions:

1. Mix together both flours, the sugar, cocoa, baking powder, salt, and baking soda in a small container .
2. In a big container, blend the whole egg and egg yolks using an electric mixer until pale and creamy, or mix thoroughly using your hands. Put in and mix in the buttermilk, melted butter, food coloring, and vanilla until well blended. Put in the dry mixture in two batches and mix using a wooden spoon only until the dough comes together. Cover and place in the fridge for minimum 2 hours or up to overnight.
3. Take the dough out of the fridge. Cover a rimmed baking sheet pan with a layer of three paper towels. Heat up 3 inches of oil using a deep pot or deep-fat fryer to 350° to 355°F.
4. As the oil heats, dust the work surface liberally with flour. Place the dough on the readied surface, coat the top of the dough slightly with flour, and roll the dough until it is ½ inch thick. Cut out donuts using a slightly floured 3-inch round cutter. Slowly gather all the left-

over dough, press it together, roll the dough again to the same thickness, and cut out as many additional donuts as you possibly can.
5. Fry multiple donuts simultaneously, without crowding. Fry approximately 1 minute and 40 seconds, turn the donuts over, and fry for approximately 1 minute and 40 seconds more, until just cooked through. With the help of a slotted spoon, take each donut out of the fryer and drain well using paper towels. Repeat the process with the rest of the dough.
6. While the doughnuts are still barely warm, spread the tops with the frosting, using a small offset spatula.

Golden Vanilla Donuts
As the name suggests, these donuts look golden, and taste like vanilla!
Yield: about eighteen 2½-inch filled round doughnuts or about sixteen 3-inch ring-shaped doughnuts
Ingredients:
- ¾ cup warm whole milk (110° to 115°F)
- ½ cup (1 stick) unsalted butter, melted and cooled slightly
- ½ cup sugar
- 7 large egg yolks, at room temperature, beaten
- 2 tablespoons pure vanilla extract
- 1 teaspoon salt
- 3 to 3¼ cups all-purpose flour
- Flavorless vegetable oil for deep-frying, such as canola
- Filling(s), topping(s), and/or glaze(s) of choice
- 1 0.25-ounce package active dry yeast

Directions:
1. Place the warm milk in a big container and sprinkle the yeast over it. Stir to combine and allow to sit for 5 minutes. In the meantime, whisk together the melted

butter, sugar, egg yolks, vanilla, and salt in a moderate-sized container.

2. Whisk the egg yolk mixture into the yeast mixture. Add mix in 3 cups of the flour; the mixture will be very wet. If using a stand mixer, attach the dough hook and mix until the dough is combined and elastic, approximately 2 minutes . You can also do this using your hands with a wooden spoon, beating rapidly for several minutes. Put in additional flour, 1 tablespoon at a time, only if necessary to create a soft, elastic dough that is still slightly sticky.

3. Put the dough in a buttered container, leaving plenty of headroom. Cover the container using plastic wrap and place in a warm, draft-free location to rise until twice its initial size, about 2 hours.

4. Softly deflate the dough, gather it into a ball again, cover with plastic again, and let rise for another 30 minutes.

5. Thoroughly flour two rimmed baking sheet pans. Softly punch down the dough and split it in half. Roll one piece of dough on a slightly floured work surface to ½-inch thickness. Cut out doughnuts with a slightly floured cutter. Use a 2½-inch round cutter for filled doughnuts or a 3-inch ring-shaped cutter for a classic doughnut shape. Repeat the process with the rest of the dough. Slowly gather all the left-over dough, press it together, roll the dough again to the same thickness, and cut out as many additional donuts as you possibly can. Place the doughnuts, well spaced, on the prepared pans. Allow to rise in a warm, draft-free location for approximately half an hour.

6. Coat two rimmed baking sheet pans with a layer of three paper towels. Heat up 3 inches of oil using a deep pot or deep-fat fryer to 350° to 355°F. Once the oil has

reached the desired temperature, fry a few doughnuts at a time; do not crowd. Fry until your donuts become slightly golden brown, approximately 1½ minutes, turn the donuts over, and fry for approximately 1½ minutes more, until the other side looks slightly golden-brown too. With the help of a slotted spoon, take each donut out of the fryer and drain well using paper towels. Repeat the process for the rest of the donuts.
7. Insert the filling(s) and/or apply dry topping(s) or glaze(s) as you wish.

Rich Crème Brûlée Donuts

The donut version of the classic crème brûlée.
Yield: about twenty-six 2½-inch filled doughnuts
Ingredients:
- 1 recipe Crispy Cream Donuts or Fundamental Yeast-Raised Donuts, prepared through the first rise

Crème brûlée pastry cream:
- ½ cup sugar
- ½ teaspoon pure vanilla extract
- 1 tablespoon unsalted butter
- 2 cups heavy cream
- 2 large eggs, at room temperature
- 2 tablespoons cornstarch
- Pinch of salt

Crème brûlée topping:
- 2 cups sugar
- Pastry bag and coupler fitted with a Bismarck #230 tip

Directions:
1. For the pastry cream: Bring the cream to a boil in a moderate-sized nonreactive saucepan over moderate heat; turn off the heat and cover to keep warm.

2. In the meantime, whisk together the eggs and sugar in a moderate-sized container until creamy. Mix in the cornstarch and salt until smooth. Pour about one-quarter of the warm cream into the egg mixture, whisking gently. Put in the remaining cream and whisk to combine. Instantly pour the mixture back into the saucepan and cook over medium-low heat. Whisk almost continuously and watch for bubbles. As soon as the mixture begins to boil, whisk rapidly and continuously over the heat for 1 to 2 minutes. The pastry cream should be thick enough to mound when dropped from a spoon, but still be satiny. Turn off the heat and whisk in the butter and vanilla.
3. Let the pastry cream cool; mix intermittently to release the heat. When it is almost at room temperature, scrape it into an airtight container, press plastic wrap directly onto the surface (to keep a skin from forming), snap on the lid, and refrigerate until thoroughly chilled, at least 4 hours and up to 2 days.
4. For the doughnuts: Thoroughly flour two rimmed baking sheet pans. Softly punch down the dough and split it in half. Roll one piece of dough on a slightly floured work surface to ½-inch thickness. Cut out doughnuts with a slightly floured 2½-inch round cutter. Repeat the process with the rest of the dough. Slowly gather all the left-over dough, press it together, roll the dough again to the same thickness, and cut out as many additional donuts as you possibly can. Place the doughnuts, well spaced, on the prepared pans. Allow to rise in a warm, draft-free location until twice its initial size, approximately half an hour.
5. Coat two rimmed baking sheet pans with a layer of three paper towels. Heat up 3 inches of oil using a deep pot or deep-fat fryer to 350° to 355°F. Once the oil has

reached the desired temperature, fry a few doughnuts at a time; do not crowd. Fry until your donuts become slightly golden brown, approximately 1½ minutes, turn the donuts over, and fry for approximately 1½ minutes more, until the other side looks slightly golden-brown too. With the help of a slotted spoon, take each donut out of the fryer and drain well using paper towels. Repeat the process for the rest of the donuts. Cool thoroughly.

6. Scrape the pastry cream into the pastry bag. Insert the tip into the side of a cooled doughnut. Squeeze the pastry bag and fill the doughnut with pastry cream only until the center of the doughnut slightly bulges. (You are aiming to pipe a generous 2 to 3 teaspoons of filling inside.) Repeat the process for the rest of the donuts and filling.

7. For the crème brûlée topping: Place the sugar in a shallow container. Coat two rimmed baking sheet pans with aluminium foil. Immerse the top of each doughnut in the sugar, gently pressing the doughnut into the sugar to encourage as much to adhere as possible. Place upright on the prepared pans. Use a teaspoon to sprinkle additional sugar on top of each doughnut. Use a propane torch to slowly and evenly melt the sugar so that it caramelizes on top of each doughnut. Alternatively, you can place the pans (one at a time) under a preheated broiler, set on high, and watch very cautiously until the sugar melts and caramelizes. Let cool to harden the sugar. These must be "bruleed" right before serving.

Rosy French Crullers

Rose water glaze on classic French crullers!
Yield: about nine 3-inch crullers
Ingredients:
- 1 recipe <u>French Crullers</u>, fried and beginning to cool
- Fresh pesticide-free rose petals

Rose water glaze:
- 1 cup sifted confectioners' sugar
- 2 tablespoons milk
- 2 teaspoons rose water

Directions:
1. Mix together the confectioners' sugar, milk, and rose water in a small container until smooth.
2. Instantly apply the glaze all over the tops of the crullers with a pastry brush or immerse the tops in the glaze. Sprinkle with rose petals while the glaze is still wet.
3. Allow to sit for 5 minutes to let the glaze set.

S'mores Donuts

The perfect donut to pack when you're going outdoors!
Yield: 10 to 12 Donuts
Total Time to Prepare: 25 Minutes
Ingredients:
- ¼ cup of butter, soft
- ¼ cup of heavy cream
- ¼ cup of water
- ½ cup of chocolate chips
- ½ cup of heavy cream
- 1 ½ cups of sugar, powdered
- 1 ½ cups of sugar, powdered
- 1 loaf of white bread
- 1 tsp. of pure vanilla

- 1, 7 ounce jar of marshmallow crème
- 2 graham crackers, crushed
- Canola oil, for frying
- Dough, frozen, thawed and risen

Directions:

1. Roll out the thawed dough on a slightly greased surface until ½ an inch in thickness. Use a biscuit cutter and cut out circles that are 2 ¾ inches in diameter. Place these dough circles onto a slightly floured baking sheet. Allow to rest for 10 minutes.
2. Then use a moderate sized container and put in the powdered sugar and water. Whisk until a smooth consistency is achieved. Set aside.
3. Fill a large stock pot with 2 to 3 inches of the canola oil. Set over moderate heat and heat up the oil until it reaches 350 degrees.
4. Stretch the dough circles with your hands and drop them into the oil. Fry for 3 minutes on each side or until golden brown. Remove and place onto a large plate lined with paper towels to drain. Repeat with the remaining dough circles.
5. Once the donuts are cooled slightly dip them into the glaze. Place onto a wire rack for the glaze to set.
6. Then make the marshmallow buttercream filling. To do this use a big container and put in the butter and marshmallow crème. Beat with an electric mixer until a smooth consistency is achieved. Put in the powdered sugar, heavy cream and pure vanilla. Beat again until smooth.
7. Put the graham crackers into a medium Ziploc bag and roll with a rolling pin to crush.
8. Make a small hole in each donut. Pour the buttercream mixture into each hole. Repeat the process with the rest of the donuts.

9. Place a small saucepan over moderate heat. Put in the heavy cream. Bring to a boil and turn off the heat. Pour over the chocolate chips and stir thoroughly until a smooth consistency is achieved. allow to thicken a little.
10. Immerse the donuts into the ganache and sprinkle the crushed graham crackers over the top. Set aside to cool a little before serving.

Saccharine Cream Donuts

Soft and sweet!

Yield: about thirty-six 2½-inch filled round doughnuts or about thirty 3-inch ring-shaped doughnuts

Ingredients:
- ¼ cup warm water (110° to 115°F)
- ½ cup flavorless vegetable oil, such as canola, plus more for deep-frying
- ½ cup heavy cream
- 6 tablespoons sugar
- ½ teaspoon salt
- ½ teaspoon freshly grated nutmeg
- ½ teaspoon pure vanilla extract
- 2½ cups boiling water
- 3 large egg yolks, well beaten
- 8 to 9 cups all-purpose flour, plus more if needed
- Filling(s), topping(s), and/or glaze(s) of choice
- 1 0.25-ounce package active dry yeast

Directions:
1. Place the warm water in a small container and sprinkle the yeast over it. Stir to combine and allow to sit for 5 minutes.
2. Place ½ cup oil, the cream, sugar, salt, nutmeg, and vanilla in a large heatproof container. Pour the boiling

water over the oil-cream mixture, whisk to combine, and let cool to lukewarm.
3. Whisk the yeast mixture and beaten egg yolks into the lukewarm mixture. Put in the flour gradually until a soft, slightly sticky, elastic dough forms. Knead thoroughly using your hands or use the dough hook of a stand mixer. Knead until the dough is elastic and pulls away from the sides of the container with a little help from a spatula. (It might still be a bit sticky and not come off cleanly on its own; do not put in more flour or the doughnuts will be dry.)
4. Put the dough in a buttered container, leaving plenty of headroom. Cover the container using plastic wrap and place in a warm, draft-free location to rise until twice its initial size, about 2 hours.
5. Thoroughly flour three rimmed baking sheet pans. Softly punch down the dough and split it into fourths. Roll one piece of dough on a slightly floured work surface to ½-inch thickness. Cut out doughnuts with a slightly floured cutter. Use a 2½-inch round cutter for filled doughnuts or a 3-inch ring-shaped doughnut cutter for a classic doughnut shape. Repeat the process with the rest of the dough. Slowly gather all the leftover dough, press it together, roll out the dough, and cut out as many additional rounds as possible. Place the doughnuts, well spaced, on the prepared pans. Allow to rise in a warm, draft-free location for 30 minutes.
6. Line three rimmed baking sheet pans with a layer of three paper towels. Heat up 3 inches of oil using a deep pot or deep-fat fryer to 350° to 355°F. Once the oil has reached the desired temperature, fry a few doughnuts at a time; do not crowd. Fry until your donuts become slightly golden brown, should take around 75 seconds, turn the donuts over, and fry for around 75 seconds

once again, until light golden-brown on the other side. With the help of a slotted spoon, take each donut out of the fryer and drain well using paper towels. Repeat with remaining doughnuts.
7. Insert filling(s) and/or apply dry topping(s) or glaze(s) as you wish.

Sizzling Cocoa Donuts

A great donut for when you're craving some hot cocoa.
Yield: 16 Donuts
Total Time to Prepare: 35 Minutes
Ingredients for the chocolate donuts:
- ¼ cup of buttermilk
- ¼ cup of vegetable oil
- ¾ cup of hot cocoa
- 1 egg, large
- 1, 16 ounce box of chocolate cake mix

Ingredients for the chocolate ganache frosting:
- ¼ cup of heavy cream
- 1 cup of chocolate, chopped
- Marshmallows, for garnish

Ingredients for the marshmallow frosting:
- ½ tsp. of pure vanilla
- 10 ounces of marshmallow fluff
- 2 cups of sugar, confectioner's
- 2 sticks of butter

Directions:
1. Add all of the ingredients for the chocolate donuts into a large bowl. Stir thoroughly until well blended.
2. Cut the donuts in half and frost the bottom halves with the frosting. Place the tops back over the frosting and pour the ganache over the top. Do at again with the rest of the.

3. Preheat the oven to 425 degrees. As the oven heats up grease a big donut pan using cooking spray.
4. Put inside the oven to bake for 8 minutes or until thoroughly baked. Take out of the oven and allow to rest on a wire rack to cool.
5. Then prepare the chocolate ganache. To do this pour the milk into a small saucepan and set over moderate heat. Bring the milk to a boil and turn off the heat. Pour the milk over the chopped chocolate. Stir thoroughly until the chocolate is fully melted.
6. Top off with the miniature marshmallows. Serve.
7. Move the donut batter into a large piping bag. Pipe the batter into the donut pan, making sure to fill each donut cup ¾ of the way full.
8. As the donuts cool make the marshmallow frosting. To do this place all of the ingredients for the frosting into a little container. Whisk until a smooth consistency is achieved.

Smooth Chocolate Donuts

Covered in sweet chocolate glaze, this recipe will make all chocolate lovers happy.
Yield: 10 Donuts
Total Time to Prepare: 20 Minutes
Ingredients for the donuts:
- ¼ cup of cocoa, powdered
- ¼ cup of milk, whole
- ¼ cup of miniature chocolate chips, optional
- ¼ cup of vegetable oil
- ¼ tsp. of salt
- ½ cup of sugar, granulated
- ½ tsp. of baker's style baking soda
- ½ tsp. of pure vanilla

- 1 cup of flour, all-purpose
- 1 egg, large
- 6 tbsp. of sour cream

Ingredients for the glaze:

- ¼ cup of milk, whole
- 1 ½ cups of sugar, powdered
- 1 tsp. of pure vanilla

Directions:

1. Preheat the oven to 375 degrees.
2. As the oven heats up use a moderate sized container and put in the all-purpose flour, granulated sugar, powdered cocoa, miniature chocolate chips and baking soda. Stir thoroughly until well blended.
3. Then use a little container and put in the pure vanilla, large egg, sour cream, whole milk and vegetable oil. Stir thoroughly until well blended. Pour into the flour mixture and stir until just blended.
4. Pour the batter into the donut pan, making sure to fill each donut cup ¾ of the way full.
5. Put inside the oven to bake for 10 mins or until the donuts are thoroughly baked. Take out of the oven and move to a wire rack to cool completely.
6. As the donuts cool make the glaze. To do this add the powdered sugar, whole milk and pure vanilla into a little container. Whisk until a smooth consistency is achieved.
7. Immerse the top side of the donuts into the glaze and place back onto the wire rack to sit for 5 minutes or until the glaze is set.

Snowy Choco-Truffle Donuts

For all the lovers of while chocolate!

Yield: depends on doughnut recipe chosen; glaze recipe makes enough to coat twenty 3-inch doughnuts

Ingredients:
- ¾ cup heavy cream
- 1 6-ounce block white chocolate, such as Valrhona Ivoire or Callebaut
- 1 recipe <u>Sour Cream Donuts</u>, <u>Traditional Buttermilk Donuts</u>, or <u>Choco-Cake Donuts</u>, cut into 3-inch rings, fried, and beginning to cool
- 21 ounces white chocolate, such as Valrhona Ivoire or Callebaut, finely chopped
- White chocolate truffle glaze:

Directions:
1. Take a sharp vegetable peeler and shave small curls off the block of chocolate directly into an airtight plastic container. These may be prepared a few days ahead and refrigerated.
2. Coat two rimmed baking sheet pans using aluminium foil or parchment paper.
3. For the glaze: Bring the cream to a simmer in a 2-quart wide saucepan over moderate heat. Turn off the heat and instantly sprinkle the chopped chocolate into the cream. Cover and allow to sit for 5 minutes. Softly mix the ganache until smooth—the heat of the cream should melt the chocolate. If the chocolate does not melt completely, place the pan over very low heat and mix the ganache frequently, until it is melted, taking care not to burn it. Cool until warm but still fluid. (You may speed up the cooling process by stirring the ganache over an ice bath. If it becomes too firm, or if you would like to return it to a softer state, simply place it over hot water or microwave it briefly.)
4. Pour the cooled glaze into a wide, shallow container. While the doughnuts are still somewhat warm, immerse

the tops in the glaze or spread the glaze using a small offset spatula. Sprinkle the glazed side generously with the white chocolate curls while the ganache is cool but still a bit sticky. Allow to sit for approximately 5 minutes to let the glaze set.

Sugar Cinnamon Donuts

An insanely delicious donut that is perfect for when you're craving something sweet.

Yield: **6 Donuts**
Total Time to Prepare: **22 Minutes**
Ingredients for the doughnuts:

- ¼ tsp. of nutmeg
- ½ tsp. of cinnamon, ground
- ½ tsp. of salt
- ¾ cup of flour, all-purpose
- 1 egg, large
- 1 tbsp. of butter, melted
- 1 tsp. of baker's style baking powder
- 1 tsp. of pure vanilla
- 1/3 cup of buttermilk
- 1/3 cup of sugar
- 2 tbsp. of cornstarch

Ingredients for topping:

- ½ cup of sugar + 1 tsp. of ground cinnamon, mixed together
- 3 tbsp. of butter, melted

Directions:

1. Take a large container and put in the all-purpose flour, cornstarch, baker's style baking powder, dash of salt, ground cinnamon and nutmeg. Stir thoroughly until well blended.

2. Take a small container and put in the buttermilk, large egg, melted butter and pure vanilla. Stir thoroughly until well blended and pour into the dry ingredients. Stir to blend.
3. Pour the batter uniformly into a big greased donut pan.
4. Put inside the oven to bake for 11 to 12 minutes at 375 degrees or until the donuts are thoroughly baked. Take out of the oven and allow to cool a little.
5. Brush both sides of the warm donuts with melted butter. Immerse in the cinnamon and sugar mixture until coated on every side. Serve.

Sweet and Sour Donuts

Lemon goes great with sugar! Don't believe me? Try these! Don't just take my word for it.

Yield: 12 Donuts

Total Time to Prepare: 20 Minutes

Ingredients for the donuts:
- ¼ cup of cornstarch
- ½ tsp. of pure vanilla
- ¾ cup of buttermilk
- ¾ cup of sugar
- 1 ¾ cup of flour, all-purpose
- 1 tbsp. of lemon juice, fresh
- 1 tsp. of salt
- 2 eggs, large and beaten
- 2 tbsp. of butter, melted
- 2 tsp. of baker's style baking powder
- 2 tsp. of lemon zest, fresh and grated

Ingredients for the coating:
- ½ cup of sugar
- 4 tsp. of lemon zest, fresh and grated
- 6 tbsp. of butter, melted

Directions:
1. Preheat the oven to 425 degrees. As the oven heats up grease two big donut pans using cooking spray.
2. Then use a big container and put in the all-purpose flour, cornstarch, sugar, baker's style baking powder and dash of salt. Stir thoroughly until blended.
3. Put in the buttermilk, large beaten eggs, melted butter, fresh lemon juice, pure vanilla and fresh lemon zest. Stir thoroughly until uniformly incorporated.
4. Pour the batter into the donut pan, making sure to fill each cup ¾ of the way full.
5. Put inside the oven to bake for 10 minutes or until the donuts are thoroughly baked. Take out of the oven and move to a wire rack to cool completely.
6. As the donuts cool use a food processor and put in the sugar and fresh lemon zest. Pulse until ground in consistency. Pour into a little container. In a different little container put in the melted butter.
7. Immerse each donut in the melted butter and then press into the lemon zest mixture. Serve while warm.

Sweet Potato Donuts

Crunchy and soft at the same time, these donuts go great with any topping!

Yield: about twelve 3-inch doughnuts

Ingredients:
- ¼ teaspoon freshly grated nutmeg
- ½ teaspoon baking soda
- ½ teaspoon ground cinnamon
- ¾ teaspoon salt
- 1 cup full-fat sour cream, at room temperature
- 1 cup lightly packed mashed sweet potato, cooled
- 1 cup sifted cake flour

- 1 cup sugar
- 1 teaspoon pure vanilla extract
- 2 large eggs, at room temperature
- 2 teaspoons baking powder
- 2½ cups all-purpose flour
- Flavorless vegetable oil for deep-frying, such as canola
- Topping(s) and/or glaze(s) of choice

Directions:
1. Mix together both flours, the baking powder, salt, baking soda, cinnamon, and nutmeg in a moderate-sized container.
2. In a big container, blend the sugar and eggs using an electric mixer until pale and creamy, or mix thoroughly using your hands. Put in and mix in the mashed sweet potato, sour cream, and vanilla just until well blended. Put in the dry mixture in two batches and mix using a wooden spoon only until the dough comes together. Cover and place in the fridge for minimum 2 hours or up to overnight.
3. Take the dough out of the fridge. Cover a rimmed baking sheet pan with a layer of three paper towels. Heat up 3 inches of oil using a deep pot or deep-fat fryer to 350° to 355°F.
4. As the oil heats, dust the work surface generously with flour. Place the dough on the readied surface, coat the top of the dough slightly with flour, and roll the dough until it is ½ inch thick. Cut out donuts using a slightly floured 3-inch round cutter. Slowly gather all the leftover dough, press it together, roll the dough again to the same thickness, and cut out as many additional donuts as you possibly can.
5. Fry multiple donuts simultaneously, without crowding. Fry until your donuts become slightly golden brown, approximately 1½ minutes, turn the donuts over, and

fry for approximately 1½ minutes more, until the other side looks slightly golden-brown too. With the help of a slotted spoon, take each donut out of the fryer and drain well using paper towels. Repeat the process for the rest of the donuts.
6. Apply dry topping(s) or glaze(s) as you wish.

Sweet Pumpkin Donuts

Are pumpkins in season? If yes, it is time to make some of these.

Yield: 12 Donuts
Total Time to Prepare: 25 Minutes
Ingredients for the donuts:
- ¼ cup + 1 tbsp. of milk, whole
- ¼ cup of brown sugar, light and packed
- ¼ cup of butter, unsalted
- ¼ tsp. of baker's style baking soda
- ½ tsp. of pumpkin pie spice
- ½ tsp. of salt
- 1 ½ tsp. of baker's style baking powder
- 1 cup of pumpkin pie filling, canned
- 2 cups of flour, all-purpose
- 2 eggs, large

Ingredients for the glaze:
- ¼ cup of butter, melted
- 1 ½ cup of sugar, powdered
- 1 tsp. of pure vanilla
- 2 tbsp. of water

Directions:
1. Preheat the oven to 325 degrees. As the oven heats up grease a two big donut pans using cooking spray.
2. Use a moderate sized container and put in the all-purpose flour, baker's style baking powder and soda,

Pumpkin spice and dash of salt. Stir thoroughly until well blended.
3. In a different moderate sized container put in the brown sugar and butter. Beat with an electric mixer until a smooth consistency is achieved. Put in the canned pumpkin whole milk and large eggs. Beat again until incorporated.
4. Pour the pumpkin mixture into the flour mixture and stir until just combined.
5. Pour the batter into the donut pan, making sure to fill each donut cup ¾ of the way full.
6. Put inside the oven to bake for 10 mins or until the donuts are thoroughly baked. Take out of the oven and move to a wire rack to cool completely.
7. As the donuts cool make the glaze. To do this melt the butter in the microwave and pour into a medium bowl. Put in the powdered sugar, water and pure vanilla. Whisk until a smooth consistency is achieved.
8. Immerse the top of the donuts into the glaze and place back onto the wire rack to sit for 5 minutes or until the glaze is set.

Toasty Almond Donuts

Almond paste tasted great in donuts!
Yield: about twenty-eight 2½-inch doughnuts
Ingredients:
- 1 recipe Crispy Cream Donuts or Fundamental Yeast-Raised Donuts, prepared through the first rise
- 2 recipes Soft and Sheer Sugar Glaze
- 22 ounces almond paste
- Flavorless vegetable oil for deep-frying, such as canola

Caramelized almonds:
- ½ cup water

- 2 ⅔ cups slivered or sliced blanched almonds, roughly chopped
- 2 cups sugar

Directions:

1. For the caramelized almonds: Cover a rimmed baking sheet pan with parchment paper or aluminium foil and coat with nonstick cooking spray. Mix the sugar and water together in a large saucepan. Bring to a simmer on moderate-high heat, swirling the pan once or twice, but do not stir. Cook (again, without stirring) until the sugar is caramelized and has turned a medium golden brown. Add mix in the almonds until coated, then instantly scrape them out onto the prepared pan. Cool and chop finely. This can be done up to 4 days ahead; store in an airtight container at room temperature.
2. Thoroughly flour two rimmed baking sheet pans. Softly punch down the dough and split it in half. Roll one piece of dough on a slightly floured work surface to ¼-inch thickness. Cut out dough rounds with a slightly floured 2½-inch round cutter. Repeat the process with the rest of the dough. Gather the scraps, press them together, roll out the dough, and cut out as many additional rounds as possible. Make sure you end up with an even number.
3. Take walnut-sized chunks of almond paste and flatten them into disks about ¼ inch thick. Place the almond paste disks in the centers of half of the dough rounds. Immerse a pastry brush in room-temperature water and lightly brush the edges of the dough around the almond paste. Place a plain round on top of each filled round and press the edges together with your fingertips to seal them well.

4. Place the doughnuts, well spaced, on the prepared pans. Allow to rise in a warm, draft-free location until twice its initial size, approximately half an hour.
5. Coat two rimmed baking sheet pans with a layer of three paper towels. Heat up 3 inches of oil using a deep pot or deep-fat fryer to 350° to 355°F. Once the oil has reached the desired temperature, fry a few doughnuts at a time; do not crowd. Fry until your donuts become slightly golden brown, approximately 1½ minutes, turn the donuts over, and fry for approximately 1½ minutes more, until light golden-brown on the other side. With the help of a slotted spoon, take each donut out of the fryer and drain well using paper towels. Repeat with remaining doughnuts.
6. While the doughnuts are still somewhat warm, immerse the tops in the glaze. Sprinkle the almonds on top while the glaze is still wet. Allow to sit for approximately 5 minutes to let the glaze set.

Traditional Lard Donuts

Classic donuts flavoured with mace!
Yield: about twenty 3-inch doughnuts
Ingredients:
- ½ a recipe Cinnamon-Sugar Topping
- ½ cup vegetable shortening, melted and slightly cooled
- ½ teaspoon salt
- 1 cup granulated sugar
- 1 cup whole milk, at room temperature
- 1 teaspoon freshly grated nutmeg
- 1 teaspoon ground mace
- 2 large eggs, at room temperature, separated
- 4 cups all-purpose flour
- 4 teaspoons baking powder

- Confectioners' sugar
- Lard for deep-frying

Directions:
1. Mix together the flour, baking powder, mace, nutmeg, and salt in a moderate-sized container .
2. In a big container, blend the granulated sugar and egg yolks using an electric mixer until well blended, or mix thoroughly using your hands. Put in and mix in the milk and the dry mixture alternately in two batches using a wooden spoon and mix only until the dough comes together. Put in and mix in the melted shortening until well blended. In a clean, grease-free container, beat the egg whites using an electric mixer or balloon whisk until soft peaks form. Fold one-quarter of the whites into the dough (the dough might be heavy, so take your time), then fold in the remaining whites.
3. Coat two rimmed baking sheet pans with a layer of three paper towels. Heat 3 inches of lard in a deep pot or deep-fat fryer to 350° to 355°F.
4. While the lard is heating, lightly cover the work surface with flour. Place the dough on the readied surface, coat the top of the dough slightly with flour, and roll the dough until it is ½ inch thick (these expand quite a bit). Cut out donuts using a slightly floured 3-inch round cutter. Slowly gather all the left-over dough, press it together, roll the dough again to the same thickness, and cut out as many additional donuts as you possibly can.
5. Fry multiple donuts simultaneously, without crowding. Fry until your donuts become slightly golden brown, approximately 1 minute and 20 seconds, turn the donuts over, and fry for approximately 1 minute and 20 seconds more, until the other side looks slightly golden-brown too. With the help of a slotted spoon, remove

each doughnut from the lard and drain well using paper towels. Repeat the process with the rest of the dough.
6. Place the cinnamon-sugar topping and confectioners' sugar in separate wide, shallow containers. While the doughnuts are still warm, toss half in the cinnamon sugar and half in the confectioners' sugar.

Traditional Powdered Donuts

This sweet donut covered with powdered sugar is perfect for satisfying your sweet tooth.

Yield: 12 Donuts
Total Time to Prepare: 15 Minutes
Ingredients:
- ¼ tsp. of nutmeg, ground
- ¾ cup of buttermilk
- ¾ cup of sugar, granulated
- 1 tsp. of salt
- 2 cups of flour cake
- 2 eggs, large and beaten
- 2 tbsp. of butter, melted
- 2 tsp. of baker's style baking powder
- Confectioner's sugar, enough for coating

Directions:
1. Preheat the oven to 425 degrees. As the oven heats up grease a big donut pan using cooking spray.
2. Use a big container and put in the cake flour, granulated sugar, baker's style baking powder, ground nutmeg and dash of salt. Stir thoroughly until well blended.
3. Put in the buttermilk, large eggs and melted butter. Whisk until thoroughly combined.
4. Pour the batter into the donut pan, making sure to fill each donut cup ¾ of the way full.

5. Put inside the oven to bake for 10 mins or until baked through. Take out of the oven and move the donuts to a wire rack to cool for 5 minutes.
6. Once cooled place the donuts in a large Ziploc bag. Fill the bag with confectioner's sugar and toss until covered. Serve.

Traditional Sour Cream Cake Donuts

This soft and sweet donut is a must-try!
Yield: 12 Donuts
Total Time to Prepare: 2 Hours
Ingredients for the donuts:
- 1 ¼ cups of sugar, granulated
- 1 tbsp. + ¾ tsp. of baker's style baking powder
- 1 tbsp. of salt
- 2 ½ tbsp. of butter
- 4 ¾ cups of flour, all-purpose
- 5 egg yolks, large
- 96 ounces of canola oil

Ingredients for the glaze:
- ½ cup of milk, whole
- 1 tsp. of salt
- 3 ¼ cups of sugar, powdered

Directions:
1. Use a big container and put in the all-purpose flour and baking powder. Put in a dash of salt and stir thoroughly to mix. Save mixture for later.
2. Use a different big container and cover with a sheet of plastic wrap. Grease the plastic wrap using cooking spray and save for later.
3. Use a big container of a stand mixer that has been fit with a paddle attachment and put in the sugar, butter and large egg yolks. Beat on the highest setting until

creamy in consistency. Put in the sour cream and continue to beat until a smooth consistency is achieved.
4. Put in the flour mixture and continue to beat on the lowermost setting.
5. Move the dough to the bowl with the greased plastic wrap. Spray the dough using cooking spray. Cover the dough with the plastic wrap and place into the refrigerator to cool for 1 hour.
6. Line a large baking sheet with a sheet of parchment paper. Spray the parchment sheet using cooking spray. Set the baking sheet aside.
7. Roll out the dough until ½ inch in thickness on a slightly greased surface. Brush the top of the dough with some flour. Cut out donut rings with a hole in the middle from the dough. Place the donuts over the readied baking sheet.
8. Coat the baking sheet with a sheet of plastic wrap. Put in the refrigerator to cool for 30 minutes.
9. During this time make the glaze. To do this use a moderate sized container and put in the whole milk, powdered sugar and a dash of salt. Whisk until a smooth consistency is achieved. Cover the glaze and save for later.
10. Pour the canola oil into a large Dutch oven and set over moderate heat. Heat up the oil until it reaches 350 degrees.
11. Add the donuts three at a time into the hot oil. Fry for 2 to 3 minutes or until golden brown. Take out and place onto a large plate covered with paper towels. Repeat the process with the rest of the. Set the donuts aside on a wire rack to cool a little.
12. Once cooled dip the donuts into the glaze and place back onto the wire rack for the glaze to set. Serve.

Ultra-Choco-Ganache Donuts

Yield: about fourteen 3-inch doughnuts

Ingredients:

- 1 recipe <u>Choco-Cake Donuts</u>, cut into 3-inch rings, fried, and beginning to cool
- 1 recipe <u>Dark Chocolate Ganache Glaze</u>
- Chocolate jimmies/sprinkles (optional)
- Chocolate shavings (optional)

Directions:

1. Immerse the top of each doughnut into the glaze or spread it using a small offset spatula. If you like, sprinkle jimmies and chocolate shavings on top of some of the doughnuts while the glaze is cool but still wet.
2. Allow to sit for approximately 5 minutes to let the glaze set.

Ultra-Sweet Fritters

These are loaded with confectioners' sugar. Make these when you are craving something sweet.

Yield: about 25 small fritters

Ingredients:

- ¼ cup granulated sugar
- ½ teaspoon pure vanilla extract
- ¾ cup sifted cake flour
- 1 cup whole-milk ricotta
- 1 teaspoon finely grated lemon zest
- 1½ teaspoons baking powder
- 2 large eggs, at room temperature
- Confectioners' sugar
- Flavorless vegetable oil for deep-frying, such as canola
- Pinch of salt

Directions:

1. Cover a rimmed baking sheet pan with a layer of three paper towels. Heat up 3 inches of oil using a deep pot or deep-fat fryer to 350° to 355°F.
2. As the oil heats, whisk together the ricotta, granulated sugar, eggs, lemon zest, vanilla, and salt in a moderate-sized container until smooth. Mix in the flour and baking powder.
3. Use a 1-inch ice cream scoop to drop the batter (carefully) into the hot oil. Alternatively, you can make small rounds by scooping a bit of dough with one teaspoon and scraping it off into the oil with another teaspoon. Fry multiple donuts simultaneously, without crowding. Fry until you see the donuts get a golden-brown colour, approximately 1 minute, turn the donuts over, and fry for approximately 1 minute more, until you see the donuts get the golden-brown colour on the other side too. With the help of a slotted spoon, remove each fritter from the oil and drain well using paper towels. Repeat the process with the rest of the dough.
4. 4. While they are still warm, coat the fritters heavily with confectioners' sugar. You can sift the sugar over them on a baking sheet pan, then roll them in excess confectioners' sugar on all sides, or you can gently toss them in a container or a bag of confectioners' sugar.

Vanilla Blast Donuts

Easy and delicious, this is the recipe you make when nothing else comes to mind.
Yield: 16 Donuts
Total Time to Prepare: 25 Minutes
Ingredients for the donuts:
- ¼ cup of butter, melted

- ¼ cup of vegetable oil
- ¼ tsp. of baker's style baking soda
- ½ cup of milk, whole
- ½ cup of sour cream
- ¾ cup of sugar, granulated
- ¾ tsp. of salt
- 1 ½ tsp. of baker's style baking powder
- 1 tsp. of nutmeg
- 2 2/3 cups of flour, all-purpose
- 2 eggs, large
- 2 tsp. of pure vanilla

Ingredients for the vanilla glaze:
- ½ cup of milk, whole
- 2 tsp. of pure vanilla
- 4 cups of sugar, powdered
- Rainbow sprinkles, for topping

Directions:
1. Preheat the oven to 425 degrees. As the oven heats up grease a big donut pan using cooking spray.
2. Then use a big container and put in the all-purpose flour, baker's style baking powder and soda, nutmeg, dash of salt and granulated sugar. Stir thoroughly until well blended.
3. Use a different moderate sized container and put in the whole milk, sour cream and large eggs. Whisk until a smooth consistency is achieved. Put in the melted butter, pure vanilla and vegetable oil. Whisk until uniformly mixed. Pour this mixture into the flour mixture and stir until just blended.
4. Pour the batter into the donut pan, making sure to fill each donut cup ¾ of the way full.
5. Put inside the oven to bake for 10 mins or until the donuts are thoroughly baked. Take out of the oven and move to a wire rack to cool completely.

6. Then make the vanilla glaze. To do this use a moderate sized container and put in the whole milk, powdered sugar and pure vanilla. Whisk until a smooth consistency is achieved.
7. Immerse the tops of each donut in the glaze and transfer to a wire rack. Sprinkle the rainbow sprinkles over the top and serve.

Vegan Gluten-Free Baked Donuts

Guest has a gluten allergy? A Vegan relative is coming over? This recipe got you covered!

Yield: twelve 3½-inch doughnuts

Ingredients:
- ⅛ teaspoon baking soda
- ¼ teaspoon freshly grated nutmeg
- ⅓ cup unsweetened applesauce
- ½ a recipe Cinnamon-Sugar Topping, made with vegan sugar
- ½ cup hot water
- ½ teaspoon salt
- ½ teaspoon xanthan gum
- ¾ cup plus 2 tablespoons vegan sugar
- 1½ teaspoons baking powder
- 1¾ cups plus 2 tablespoons sifted glutenfree baking mix, such as Bob's Red Mill All-Purpose Baking Flour
- 3 tablespoons pure vanilla extract

Directions:
1. Position a rack in the middle of the oven. Preheat the oven to 325°F. Coat two standard-sized doughnut pans (12 wells total) with nonstick cooking spray.
2. Mix together the flour, baking powder, salt, xanthan gum, nutmeg, and baking soda in a big container .

3. Mix together the sugar, water, applesauce, and vanilla in a moderate-sized container. Pour the wet ingredients over the dry mixture and fold together using a wooden spoon just until well blended and smooth. Divide the batter evenly among the wells of the prepared pans. Use a small offset spatula to spread the batter evenly, if needed.
4. Bake until a toothpick inserted in the center of a doughnut shows a few moist crumbs when removed, approximately 12 minutes. Cool the pans on racks for about 5 minutes, and then unmold the doughnuts directly onto the racks.
5. While the doughnuts are still warm, toss them in the cinnamon sugar until completely coated.

Vibrant Donuts

The colourful donuts are sweetly delicious, and you can never go wrong with them.

Yield: 14 Donuts

Total Time to Prepare: 20 Minutes

Ingredients for the donuts:
- ¼ tsp. of salt
- ½ cup of butter
- ¾ cup of buttermilk
- 1 ½ tsp. of baker's style baking powder
- 1 ¾ cup of flour, all-purpose
- 1 tbsp. of cornstarch
- 1 tsp. of pure vanilla
- 2 eggs, large and beaten
- 2/3 cup of sugar

Ingredients for the glaze:
- 1 tsp. of pure vanilla
- 2 cups of sugar, powdered

- 3 to 4 tbsp. of milk, whole
- Food coloring, your favorite

Directions:
1. Preheat the oven to 350 degrees. As the oven heats up grease two donut pans using cooking spray.
2. Take a large container and put in the all-purpose flour, cornstarch, baker's style baking powder and dash of salt. Stir thoroughly until well blended.
3. Use a different big container and put in the butter and sugar. Beat with an electric mixer until a smooth consistency is achieved. Put in the large eggs and pure vanilla. Beat again until incorporated.
4. Add the butter and sugar mixture into the flour mixture. Stir thoroughly until blended. Pour in the buttermilk and stir thoroughly until a smooth consistency is achieved.
5. Pour the batter into the donut pan, making sure to fill each donut cup ¾ of the way full.
6. Put inside the oven to bake for 10 to 12 minutes or until golden brown. Take out of the oven and move to a wire rack to cool fully.
7. While it cooks, make the glaze. To do this use a moderate sized container and put in the powdered sugar, whole milk and pure vanilla. Whisk until a smooth consistency is achieved.
8. Separate the glaze into separate little containers. Put in a few drops of your favorite food coloring into each bowl and stir thoroughly until the color is beautiful.
9. Immerse the cooled donuts into the desired colored glaze and place back onto a wire rack to sit until the glaze is set. Serve.

1.

Walnaple Donuts

Walnuts go great with maple glaze!
Yield: about twenty-four 2½-inch doughnuts
Ingredients:

Walnut streusel:
- ¼ cup granulated sugar
- 1 large egg white
- 1 teaspoon ground cinnamon
- 1½ cups walnut halves, finely chopped

Donuts:
- ½ teaspoon baking soda
- 1 cup full-fat sour cream, at room temperature
- 1 cup granulated sugar
- 1 cup plus 1 tablespoon sifted cake flour
- 1 tablespoon baking powder
- 1 teaspoon ground cinnamon
- 1 teaspoon pure vanilla extract
- 1 teaspoon salt
- 2 large eggs, at room temperature
- 2½ cups all-purpose flour
- 6 tablespoons (¾ stick) unsalted butter, melted and cooled
- Flavorless vegetable oil for deep-frying, such as canola

Maple glaze:
- 2 cups sifted confectioners' sugar
- 3 tablespoons pure maple syrup
- 4 tablespoons water

Directions:
1. For the streusel: Preheat the oven to 325°F. Cover a rimmed baking sheet pan with parchment paper. Whisk

the egg white in a small container until frothy. Mix in the granulated sugar and cinnamon; fold in the nuts. Spread the mixture on the prepared pan in a thin, even layer. Bake until the mixture is beginning to dry, approximately 10 minutes. Stir to break up the nuts. Continue to bake until the nut mixture is golden brown, approximately 5 minutes more. Cool the pan completely on a rack. Transfer the streusel to a cutting board and chop very finely. Transfer to a wide, shallow container.
2. For the doughnuts: Mix together both flours, the baking powder, cinnamon, salt, and baking soda in a moderate-sized container .
3. In a big container, blend the granulated sugar and eggs using an electric mixer on medium-high speed until pale and creamy, or mix thoroughly using your hands. Put in and mix in the melted butter, sour cream, and vanilla until well blended.
4. Put in the dry mixture in two batches and mix using a wooden spoon only until the dough comes together. Cover and place in the fridge for minimum 2 hours or up to overnight.
5. Take the dough out of the fridge. Coat two rimmed baking sheet pans with a layer of three paper towels. Heat up 3 inches of oil using a deep pot or deep-fat fryer to 350° to 355°F.
6. As the oil heats, lightly cover the work surface with flour. Place the dough on the readied surface, coat the top of the dough slightly with flour, and roll out to ¾-inch thickness. Cut out doughnuts with a slightly floured 2½-inch round cutter. Slowly gather all the left-over dough, press it together, and cut out as many additional doughnuts as possible.
7. Fry multiple donuts simultaneously, without crowding. Fry until your donuts become slightly golden brown,

approximately 1 minute, turn the donuts over, and fry for approximately 1 minute more, until the other side looks slightly golden-brown too. With the help of a slotted spoon, take each donut out of the fryer and drain well using paper towels. Repeat the process with the rest of the dough.
8. For the glaze: Mix the confectioners' sugar and maple syrup in a small saucepan. Put in 3 tablespoons of the water and whisk until smooth, adding the remaining 1 tablespoon water if needed to make a thick but smooth and pourable glaze. Heat the mixture gently over low heat until very warm to the touch but not hot. Turn off the heat and scrape into a wide, shallow container.
9. While the doughnuts are still somewhat warm, immerse the tops in the glaze, then quickly immerse the glazed side into the streusel. Arrange the doughnuts, streusel side up, on a rack for minimum 30 minutes or longer if necessary to set the glaze and topping.

Endnote

All sweet things must come to an end. A donut doesn't last forever, and neither does a book. The important thing is to make most of the good things while they last.

Use the recipes in this book as a base to build upon your own foundation. You are the only one who can make the perfect donut for you. Experiment with your favourite ingredients and come up with new recipes.

Cooking is a playground where there are no rules. Go wild! And don't forget to have fun!

Marissa Marie

Made in the USA
Monee, IL
03 December 2020